SEMIOTEXT(E) INTERVENTION SERIES

Published with support from Mexico's National Fund for
Culture and the Arts and its National Arts Creators System,
2011–2013.

Published by Semiotext(e)
2007 Wilshire Blvd., Suite 427, Los Angeles, CA 90057
www.semiotexte.com

Translation Editor: Gabriela Jauregui

Thanks to John Ebert, Ben Ehrenreich, Jen Hofer, Daniel
Hernandez, Marco Vera and Sarah Wang.

Design: Hedi El Kholti

ISBN: 978-1-58435-110-8
Distributed by The MIT Press, Cambridge, Mass.
and London, England
Printed in the United States of America

Sergio González Rodríguez

The Femicide Machine

Translated by Michael Parker-Stainback

semiotext(e)
intervention
series □ 11

Contents

Introduction

BORDER AND VECTOR

In Ciudad Juárez, a territorial power normalized barbarism. This anomalous ecology mutated into a femicide machine: an apparatus that didn't just create the conditions for the murders of dozens of women and little girls, but developed the institutions that guaranteed impunity for those crimes and even legalized them. A lawless city sponsored by a State in crisis. The facts speak for themselves.

Ciudad Juárez represents the kind of human settlement that results from the destabilizing tensions of geopolitical interest. World order reveals its greatest contradictions there. Located in the Mexican state of Chihuahua, Ciudad Juárez lies in the middle of the borderland that unites Mexico and the United States: an American vector of oil fields, natural gas, solar and wind-energy exploitations, and first-class military bases and installations.

The history of Ciudad Juárez evolved asynchronously. Bordering El Paso, Texas, the city has been subject to rapid modernization and industrialization processes over the last fifty years; processes determined by economic and political power structures that oscillate between the formal and the informal, the legal and the illegal. This alegality allowed for the inclusion of organized crime within the city, accompanied in turn by its perverse effects: institutional corruption and impunity for criminals.

This development mode—a global, pragmatic production complex based on a depredation of the labor force in the name of the highest profit—unleashed intense population growth. Migrants arrived in Ciudad Juárez in search of work, and at the same time, local birth rates remained high.

The immediate consequences of this growth were increased poverty, marginalization, and a scarce quality of life. The city's cluster of institutions was incapable of providing satisfactory levels of housing, healthcare, safety, transportation, education, justice, culture, and environmental quality. Above all, they were unable to create a framework of respect for human rights.

By placing the *maquila*, or assembly industry, at the center of the border model, Ciudad Juárez became a city-machine whose tensions entwined Mexico, the United States, the global economy and the underworld of organized crime. These tensions were inscribed both in the overall operations of the city and in the concentric, ultra-contemporary terrain of its environment: The collective and personal tempo of Ciudad Juárez is linked to the simultaneous, ubiquitous reach of the global economy and its information and communication technologies.

The 1991 announcement of the North American Free Trade Agreement (NAFTA) between the US, Mexico, and Canada would accelerate the city-machine's functioning and its recharged iteration: the femicide machine.

To understand the use of the compound term *femicide machine* as it relates to Ciudad Juárez, one must go beyond the simple metaphor of an industrial city. The femicide machine is inscribed within a particular structure of the neo-Fordist economy. In other words, it is a parasite of this structure, just as the structure itself was encrusted upon the Mexican border. The structure is defined by mass economic regulation on an international, macroeconomic scale, and by an assembly line production that differentiates products via flexible, automated methods, information technology, and specially categorized labor. This economic set-up presents a new, complex, interconnected spectrum of procedures for exploiting material and human resources, while at the same time maintaining more traditional mechanisms of exploitation. These procedures are both tangible and intangible, and their ramifications are global.

The femicide machine has characteristics that differ from the structure that supports it, and it also remains distinct from the State it inhabits. It derives strength from this autonomy, which makes fighting it difficult, because the machine tends to multiply, or to transform in an expanded, specialized reproduction of itself.

Ciudad Juárez's femicide machine can be better understood in light of a generic description of the ultra-contemporary machine: "The machine is not limited to managing and striating entities closed off to one another, but opens up to other machines and, together with them, moves machinic assemblages. It consists of machines and penetrates several structures simultaneously. It depends on external elements in order to be able to exist at all."[1] It is a generator that creates and directs non-lineal aspects, potential dimensions and unprecedented qualities.

This machinic integrity is complemented by the human (individual, group, or collective) element that devised it, keeps it running, and at some point, can destroy it. It also maintains differentiated links and exchanges with other machines, real and virtual: the war machine, the police machine, the criminal machine, or the machine of apolitical conformity.

Ciudad Juárez's femicide machine is composed of hatred and misogynistic violence, *machismo*, power and patriarchal reaffirmations that take place at the margins of the law or within a law of complicity between criminals, police, military, government officials, and citizens who constitute an a-legal old-boy network. Consequently, the machine enjoys discrete protection from individuals, groups, and institutions that in turn offer judicial and political impunity, as well as supremacy over the State and the law.

The femicide machine applies its force upon institutions via direct action, intimidation, ideological sympathy, inertia, and indifference. This prolongs its own dominance, and guarantees its own unending reproducibility. Traced over time, its effects recreate its *modus operandi*: In Ciudad Juárez, violence against women multiplied for more than ten years, while at the same time a veil of impunity was constructed. In subsequent years, disdain for and oblivion of the victims became more formalized through political institutions, the judicial system, and the mass media. The price of this misfortune was paid within the border territory more than anywhere else.

In the past half-century, Ciudad Juárez gave birth to four cities in one: the city as a northern

Mexican border town/United States' backyard; the city inscribed in the global economy; the city as a theater of operations for the war on drugs; and the femicide city. Extreme capitalism converges here: plutocratic, corporate, monopolistic, global, speculative, wealth-concentrating, and predatory, founded on military machinations and media control. Ciudad Juárez is the realization of planned speculation that practices on city-slums and on the people there who are considered of little value. The human cannon fodder suffer while trying to reverse the adverse situation of living in cities at constant risk or in continuous crisis, and facing community disintegration.

The femicide machine has affected the entire urban-territorial space of Ciudad Juárez. The criminals who operate it have made the extent of their crimes so blatantly clear that they can only be read as a generalized attack on order and the rules of coexistence.

Originally, the land that comprised Ciudad Juárez was private: The city's growth has been achieved through government-sanctioned capitalist real-estate developments, squatting, and self-construction on behalf of inhabitants. Systematic actions against women bear the signs of a campaign: They smack of turf war, of the land's rape and subjugation. These acts imply a strategic re-territorialization, as real as it is symbolic, that includes capital property (contractors, shopping centers, industrial parks, basic services) and the possession of public space through ubiquitous occupation. Ultimately, what is expressed is the sovereign authority to determine urban life at the cost of the citizenry's slow and steady impoverishment.

The femicide machine has achieved its capacity for control, domination, vigilance, and espionage within Ciudad Juárez through institutional corruption and the rise of criminal industries. The US border itself has become vulnerable, and the menace against it grows day after day. This machine has left traces of its crimes on streets, crossroads, neighborhoods, industrial parks, and specific urban and suburban zones by throwing the bodies of dozens of victims there. Messages, wounds, marks, mutilation, and torture have been inscribed on these bodies: practices that reveal a shift from sociopathy to unlimited psychopathy, fed by institutional shortages and the fruits of impunity. The destructive impulse becomes automatic.

Authorities manipulated facts in order to avoid responsibilities; women were revictimized. The murdered women were accused of somehow having collaborated with their victimizers. The gravity of these events was minimized by attributing the murders to family dysfunctionality; as a standard, the victims were associated with organized crime. Members of the victims' family circles and other innocent parties were groundlessly accused of the murders. Every tossed, buried, and half-buried corpse offered a glimpse of the perimeter of an ominous totality—the grid of a vast and expansive power. Media and trans-media space channeled these messages to the entire world. It is possible that other femicide machines are now gestating in other Mexican cities and elsewhere on the planet.

1

BORDER TOWN/BACKYARD

The mountains, sand, and city of Ciudad Juárez are a rusty metallic color, absorbent and splintering, yellowish-brown in the summer, leaden and gray in the winter. Sand floats in the air. At other times, it sticks in your teeth: Its taste repels, intrigues, attracts. In any case, it's unavoidable. In spring, the sun glints and freezing wind blows. At those times, the city is swept by a cloud of dust eventually drowned by the rain. Avenues and streets become torrential rapids and mud slides that the desert soon devours.

One hundred and four degree heat, winter cold hovering around zero degrees, fierce winds, sprawling neighborhoods, minimal basic services, vacant lots, abandoned housing, broken sewers and water mains, traffic circulating day and night along desolate roads. On either side of these roads, there are never-ending homesteads of people who stick it out and make life or survival plans—a transversal existence.

South of the border crossing and the old red-light district, with its nightclubs, *cantinas* and bars lies the *zona dorada*—the golden zone—the city's most urbanized area. Its avenues recreate the broad strokes of US-style cities. Suddenly, the rectilinear order of these avenues twists off in an unexpected direction. A saturation of outdoor advertising appears with loud colors, along with a scattering of brands: a parody of a Texan city. At once contemporary and anachronistic, vital and decadent, Ciudad Juárez looks like a collage. The half-century old promise of the city as a thriving business and recreational zone rests in suspended animation. Signs of underground violence suddenly emerge on street corners, walls, uprooted fence posts, and sidewalks torn up by car crashes, decay and damage caused by fire, graffiti tags, bullet holes. An invisible and encompassing menace floats there.

Ciudad Juárez sprawls in conflicting directions: extensive, haphazard, discontinuous, and precarious. Unlike other human settlements where urbanized areas outnumber the slums, the outskirts of Ciudad Juárez are larger than its center. This center enjoys the basic urban services expected in high-income neighborhoods, but infrastructure decreases as the neighborhoods expand outward, except in the case of industrial parks.

Known as Ciudad Juárez since 1888, the former *Paso del Norte* was home to a mission during Mexico's colonial period. Since then, it has been the territory of indigenous people in the process of extinction; of immigration, transience, contraband, and often, acute violence. To the north lies the border, mountains lie to the west, and the desert—an area of expansion—lies to the south. The informal, or underground economy and its way of life are part of the city's history, and its stigma of being a city that lives in perpetual dusk. During the last half of the twentieth century, Ciudad Juárez became associated with multinational industrial production and cutting-edge technology. Simultaneously, Ciudad Juárez's importance as a drug trafficking corridor grew.

Since the first years after the Mexican Revolution (1910–1921), the city developed a tourist and leisure industry whose nexus was uncontrolled migration. Prohibition in the United States (1919–1933) drove those seeking escape from regulations south of the border. Organized crime awaited with offers of sex, booze, and drugs. During these years, Mexico was experiencing a period of adjustment after the armed conflict between the central government and the nation's states. Far away from the nation's center in Mexico City, Ciudad Juárez reaffirmed its regional pride.

The city grew in the 1940s thanks to sex tourism, commerce, and migratory flow. During World War II, soldiers from the military base in Fort Bliss, Texas, spent their time off from duty in the Mexican city.

The 1950s were the golden age of Ciudad Juárez's nightlife fame. The city became a fleeting space where the US tourist could dream of having a Mexican prostitute and, by symbolic displacement, all of Mexico for a moment. An extension of the Santa Fe international bridge to El Paso, Texas, Avenida Juárez became a brittle, colorful stage: a film location that tried to mask the barbarity of the border while remaining true to the city's tradition of delivering low-cost sexual services and entertainment.

Small local industries that supplied basic goods such as soap, oils, and threads began to decline. At the beginning of the 1960s, Mexico's federal government created the National Border (1961) and Border Industrialization (1965) programs— programs that rapidly lead to the establishment of the *maquila*, or manufacturing-assemblies. Built with foreign capital, these factories provide cheap labor to manufacture or assemble assorted parts of a product destined for exportation.

And so Ciudad Juárez became a magnet for labor along Mexico's northern border during the last decade of the twentieth century. The critical decade. The 2000 census registered a population of 1,218,000. Ten years before, less than 800,000 people resided in Ciudad Juárez. The population tripled between 1970 and 2000, and 40 percent of this population lived in extreme poverty, without basic urban services, on the margins of society. By 1995, an estimated 300 newcomers reached Ciudad Juárez each day, and the city maintained a transient, or floating, population of 250,000. Ciudad Juárez was the preferred gateway for Mexicans traveling to Texas and New Mexico. Forty-two million people and seventeen million vehicles were estimated to have crossed the Ciudad Juárez/El Paso border in 1996. New Mexico's State Land Office considered it one of the busiest borders for human transit in the world. Fluidity grew as a binational dilemma.

Ciudad Juárez suffered the effects of both nations' economic asymmetry: population explosion compounded by a lack of infrastructure and basic services, the despoiling of natural resources, water shortages (with some 15 percent of its water supply lost to waste) and alarming pollution from industrial waste, automobiles, and the city's some 300 brickworks. By 1999, it was Mexico's fourth most polluted city. Little has improved since.

The city was plagued with excess automobiles, a substantial number of them castoffs from the US. Eighty percent of in-city travel was conducted in private cars, around 307,000. While only 37 percent of Mexico City residents owned cars, in Ciudad Juárez, car ownership reached 70 percent. Auto theft abounded, as did *yonques*—auto junkyards or scrap yards. The most common crimes committed by young people were auto theft and possession of stolen vehicles. A mobile society emerged and with it, the widespread use of cell phones. Almost half of Ciudad Juárez's population used them, compared to the rest of Mexico where coverage reached little more than 15 percent. Cell phone use during the 1990s in Ciudad Juárez was comparable to that of some European nations. But the synergy between people and machines in Ciudad Juárez is singular: the distinctive trait of an urban, adaptable, and nomadic sensibility.

By the end of the twentieth century, Ciudad Juárez encapsulated the hardships of a border city. Its rapid demographic growth and lack of infrastructure, services, and quality of life occurred within an institutional context where informal economies—like contraband and goods piracy, the underground economies of drugs, arms and human trafficking, money laundering, extortion, theft, prostitution, and child/teen exploitation—were interconnected with the formal economy.

Because of its asynchronous historical development, Ciudad Juárez contained an amalgam of premodern, modern and ultramodern zones that, around 1990, were being inserted into a new network of global economic relations and information societies. Conditions were set for the rise of the femicide machine.

Ciudad Juárez is scarred by cultural differences. The condemnation of Hispanics as an inquisitorial culture, ignorant and resistant to change, persists in the US. Ideologically, the valorization of WASP culture has persisted at the forefront of US imperialist thrusts. The Toynbee-Spengler-Huntington triad is still in effect, enthroning Protestant morality: the search for social perfection via the imposition of norms. At the nucleus of this discourse, war appears as an inevitable historical motor, stemming from cultural differences. From this perspective, Western culture within the US and non-Hispanic Europe is seen as the paragon of accomplishment. Everything else, including the Hispanic world (i.e. Spain, Mexico, Central, and South America) is a "sub-civilization." In this context, Ciudad Juárez becomes the gateway to a Mexican hell: a subject for extreme tourism and yellow journalism.[1] The world reduced to a crime tabloid article.

Within the framework of violence in the Americas, the implications of this US perspective can be seen operating on two levels: first, the geo-political vision of the US as it enters the 21st century; and second, the theater of US military operations on the subcontinent. The objectives are to incite violence, tension, and social crises in which arms stockpiling and paramilitarization sustain the political formality of Latin American countries in strategic zones.

In relation to Western predominance, Latin Americans and Hispanics (or Latinos in the US)—be they immigrants or not—comprise a secondary population vis à vis the "occidental" majority: an estate prone to disorder that needs to be controlled. Even now, the stigma attached to Hispanic people and culture persists, and its influence shapes contemporary events. Ideologies can be measured less by their stated values than by the principles of efficacy and prejudice that lend them validity. Questioning this anti-Hispanic ideology is important, because these beliefs resist erosion.

Ciudad Juárez suffers from its asymmetrical relation to El Paso, Texas. It represents a "backyard" city for the US: a metaphor for private territoriality and subsidiary domain. The dump-desert city, the metropolis in ruins where human-machine-beasts, vacant lots, and junk survive as a generalized condemnation: the kingdom of rust that moves along a slithering plane, a pure materiality no longer thinkable now that the norms and procedures of the city's past tend to be nothing more than post-human information. In Juárez, the fluidity of years gone by is now halted by army checkpoints, police, gunfire, gated communities, and the anti-violence protests of its citizens.

Ever since the hip-hop song "Carlitos" was nominated for the top prize in the 2009 Juárez Hip-Hop Awards, the musical group MC Crimen has seen its fame grow along the Mexican border. At the awards ceremony held at a local bar, one of the most powerful expressions of urban youth culture against brutality was heard. Besides MC Crimen, some of the most notable bands in hip hop include groups such as Delezeta (DLZ), Versenarios, and Escuadrón Kon Clase, among many others. This is the music young people listen to in a climate of violence.

These rappers' music projects represent a generational alternative to traditional *corrido* songs that celebrate drug trafficking, its leaders, and their activities. And while the themes taken on by young people in border hip-hop contain diverse content, most still use storytelling or ironies that refer to everyday events. This is how they establish connections among different musicians and audiences to configure a collective, local-impact response.

According to the United Nations, one billion people live in degraded slums around the world. Half of these people are younger than 24 years old.[2] It is estimated that by 2030, the poor and marginalized population living on the outskirts and slums will have doubled.[3] They are the victims of environmental devastation, violence, pandemic disease, drug trafficking, terrorism, and labor and sexual exploitation. Rap and hip-hop have become the most important cultural expression for the world's poor and marginalized youth. Through the sponsorship of UN-Habitat, programs such as Messengers of Truth have emerged to bring these young people together at concerts, recording sessions, and other rap and hip-hop related activities in Latin America, Asia, and Africa.

MC Crimen sings: "Another day dawns and Carlitos turns 13 today/his father wasn't there to congratulate him/give him a hug/since he hit the alleys/he's been looking pretty thin/his mom doesn't have time to raise him right/because she works all day/fighting so he won't go without anything/struggling so he can have everything/he left school to hang out/what a sad childhood he had/when shots broke out in his 'hood/he ended up dead on the ground/all too young/he went to his grave."[4] MC Crimen is similar to groups like Bogotá's Santa Mafia.

Violence in Ciudad Juárez is connected to Mexico's institutional degradation. Government plans for Ciudad Juárez have been limited to minimal improvements (schools, sports fields, family support, etc.) that do not begin to contemplate the problem as a whole. Specifically, the plans do not contemplate the problem of public safety:

more police or security officers promise nothing, except more of what has not worked. The government's response ignores the central concern: the reconstruction of the political and economic fabric of a city, devastated by symbiosis between local power, drug traffickers, and US interests. "Listen look and shut up/or you'll die from the bullets of a ma-ma-chine gun," MC Crimen sings. The citizens of Ciudad Juárez demand more culture and less violence. In 2010 there were more than 3000 executions there.

ASSEMBLY/GLOBAL CITY

Just south of the United States, Mexico's border towns witnessed the growth of the manufacturing-assembly model at the end of the twentieth century. In 1969, Mexico ranked first among manufacturing-assembly countries. By 1996, 372 of these businesses employed nearly 222,000 laborers, primarily in the automotive and electronics sectors. A large part of this work force came from the states of Sinaloa, Durango, Coahuila, Zacatecas, Aguascalientes, and from southern Chihuahua. For the first time since the emergence of the *maquila* industry, male employees outnumbered female employees, who for years had provided specialized productivity, and a malleable, disciplined, and efficient workforce.

Ciudad Juárez is home to some ten major industrial developments, which create a social bipolarity. On one side, there are highly skilled, high-wage, transnational, cosmopolitan workers who enjoy ample spending power. On the other, there are common, low-wage laborers. Ciudad Juárez's central area features well-constructed buildings, street fixtures, signage, and landscaping: an architectural style that favors concrete, brick, steel, glass, air-conditioning, privacy, and extensive surveillance systems—guardhouses, video cameras, closed-circuit television, and barbed or electrified fencing—a new aesthetic of social prestige, protecting its occupants from the dangers the rest of the population suffers.[1] The impulse behind this form of building is to appropriate public space. Upscale neighborhoods now favor private streets and gated communities. Urban life is reduced to the notion of the "container," like the containers used for storing and shipping merchandise. The city: a container of containers. And surrounding this, a multiplicity of poorly finished brick housing, fashioned from discarded and shoddy materials, sprouts up in semi-vacant, unfinished neighborhoods lacking paved roads and basic services. These neighborhoods are subject to the domination of both common and organized crime.

The manufacturing-assembly industry in Ciudad Juárez has stretched out and absorbed the entire city, restructuring its form and imprinting the dynamics of socio-cultural segregation upon each class of inhabitants, whether or not they are employed by the industry. This dynamic is the result of both the strength and strategy exercised by multinational corporations, which prosper from urban impoverishment in developing nations. By engaging in factory work, each worker experiences and subjectivizes corporate power, and ends up making that power part of his or her daily life: control, discipline, a model of architectural-industrial surveillance, and functionalism extends into their bodies and private lives.

Since the city developed around the manufacturing-assembly plants and the industrial parks that house them, public space became ordered around the plants. The industry molded development and determined the actions taken by local investors and government. Industrial processes work to the detriment of people, both collectively as well as individually, within the domain of their bodies. This is especially true for women, who have come to provide a source of labor and maintenance while remaining the mainstay of the family. Women— above all, working women—moved into the role of the urban protagonist, a role as direct as it was subliminal. The presence of women in the home, on the street, in factories, and in spaces used for relaxation and leisure unleashed men's hatred.

Civil coexistence turned into gender harassment and aggression. A risk group—working women, girls, female students, and young women looking for work—emerged within the urban territory, inhabiting dangerous zones and corridors. In the absence of a framework of gender equality, relationships of power and exploitation, asymmetry, and contradiction were imposed. The population incarnates a human terrarium for the *maquiladoras* that congregate in the city. Bio-political territory *par excellence*: the body as the objective of power.

Manufacturing-assembly in Ciudad Juárez came to be characterized by the search for maximum quality control and the use of multifunctional labor, robotics, and automation. This ultracontemporary model filtered into a collective understanding of the role of the economic and the social within the city, moving from the industrial sphere to the public arena. The result was disorder, which in turn unfolded into dissolution as it extended into the domestic realm. In the contrasts and folds between efficiency and degradation violence is born.

As an industry, manufacturing-assembly imposes stability, and in doing so, it establishes numerous understandings, both individually and collectively. Above all, manufacturing-assembly—*la maquila*—becomes a symbol, and the conduct within it attains a productive ritual status, similar in many ways to ancient societies' rituals regarding the sacred.[2] Deep inside the factory, female laborers carry out repetitive, reflective, compulsive, integrating, stylized, collective, and generative tasks, immersed in the connective plurality of the manu-facturing-assembly plant and its "just-in-time" work tempo. This ritualization of labor ultimately integrates female and male workers into the production space. In exchange, they allow themselves to be assimilated into the productive apparatus in an endless flux of sacrifice and self-sacrifice.

A factory that assembles or manufactures products for export within a neo-Fordist model in Ciudad Juárez is different from an analogous factory in a developed city. Manufacturing-assembly along the Mexican border exists as an ultra-contemporary technological enclave in the midst of a degraded environment. In comparable European facilities, for example, both the plant and its working conditions feature "state-of-the-art" technology.[3] At once a theater and a museum, this "transparent factory" seeks to project cleanliness and an environmental equilibrium among a population that enjoys a high quality of life. The opaque Ciudad Juárez factory is its opposite: a corral and amphitheater whose immediate surroundings are polluted, broken, violent, and unstable; a visual allusion to the darkness reproduced by patriarchal domination which is deceitful, harassing and aggressive:[4] The cubed or rectangular space, produced amid abject urbanism.

The opaque factory constitutes a dual micro-cosm, uniting the disciplinary-productive with the abject-dissolvent within its urban context. A human resources officer who has worked at numerous *maquiladoras* testified: "No one wants to talk about the high drug consumption levels inside industrial plants, or about the drug trade that takes place in factories. Employees sell cocaine to their coworkers to withstand work pressure or double shifts. Female employees also suffer other types of abuse. I've seen men in high positions of authority 'raffle off' the most attractive young female employees. Looking through tinted office windows facing the factory floor, they would choose the girls and then, in the best cases, sexually harass them."[5] The industrial assembly plant as a space of masculine concentration.

Examples of abject architecture: extermination camps, collapsible garrison houses or blockhouses, bunkers, and criminal/political torture chambers. The opaque factory would be, at its extreme, the femicide machine's antechamber, an exceptional "camp," as described by Agamben: "Inasmuch as its inhabitants have been stripped of every political status and reduced completely to naked life, the camp is also the most absolute biopolitical space that has ever been realized—a space in which power confronts nothing other than pure biological life without any mediation."[6] Contemporary biopolitics are executed in these spaces, and under this power, life—stripped of all rights—becomes the object of exploitation and death experiments.

In the 1990s, Ciudad Juárez achieved Mexico's lowest unemployment rate and maintained the largest number of manufacturing-assembly workers in the country. The individual here becomes a prosthesis, a kind of cyborg working beneath the most vertical form of command for a pittance. In the last twenty years, wages in Mexico have lost over 75 percent of their value: an insuperable hardship. The 2008 world economic crisis provoked factory closings.[7] In 2000 there were 264,700 manufacturing-assembly jobs. Ten years later, 339 assembly plants remained, offering some 199,800 jobs.[8] The remaining plants profited from the economic leverage and labor force, which ensured the survival of a productive enclave whose functions depended upon multinational commerce (ninety-seven percent of its raw materials come from outside Mexico). The violence and social insecurity experienced in recent years have only affected the service sector and local businesses.

During the first decade of the twenty-first century, Mexico became the world's cheapest country for industrial assembly.[9] When conditions in China improved due to reformist policy, Mexico undersold its labor. Linked to the United States, the world's largest superpower, Mexico clings to a retrograde logic based on demographic excess and an overflowing workforce that exceeds the market's ability to employ it. Eighty-four and a half percent of Mexican exports are destined for the us market. Mexico: the asymmetric partner.

Mexico's unequal distribution of wealth and its cyclical economic crises have reduced access to means of minimum well-being for most individuals. An urban nation that has wholly abandoned its rural profile, Mexico's population is clustered in cities or in migrant populations. The median age of Mexico's population was 22 at the dawn of the twenty-first century. Lacking employment and living amidst the educational system's failures, young people are exposed to the night brigades: delinquency and organized crime; the informal, underground economy and underemployment.

Violence against women in Ciudad Juárez maintained a particular character at the end of the twentieth century. Along that part of the border, the crime of rape affected mostly females, but it also affected males. Between 1996–1999, 20 percent of rape victims were male. The majority of these victims were younger than 10 and were raped by their fathers or stepfathers. Poor, broken, uneducated families. Child victims of rape tend to become potential rapists. In subsequent years, women became the object of many forms of masculine violence, which came to be ubiquitous; violence due to multiple institutional, sociological, and psychological causes. Attacks against women were explained within the context of these traditional problems. The dominant patriarchal ideology, borne of religion, prevails in explaining the sociological context.

In Ciudad Juárez, the masculine perception that every woman is merely a sexual object results when stereotypes surrounding the "pure woman" —wife and mother—are exhausted. A woman who works and has no need for masculine protection becomes the antithesis of the "pure woman" fantasy. Once freed from financial dependence upon male family members—and from a very young age, even following puberty—women are identified as dirty; interested only in money, sex, and fun during her leisure time. A circle of hatred is closed and violence is unleashed: a situation that moves from the body to territory.

The use, management, and possession of Ciudad Juárez's public space as it relates to the murder of women is inscribed not just in the decisions of groups that carry out a-legal—between licit and illicit—violence, but also in strategies of territorial domination around the border: in the origins of capital and growth, in urban development, and among contractors, real estate speculators, and within the *maquila* industry. A few families enjoy generational fortunes made in big businesses, such as nightclubs, beer, liquor and soft-drink sales monopolies, shopping centers, industrial developments, hospitals, basic infrastructure services, and in the media.

In Ciudad Juárez, public space has owners before it has temporary occupants.

Lomas de Poleo, for example, one of the sites where various bodies of murdered women have been discovered, is a neighborhood within the *Anapra* zone. This zone consists of almost 177,668,769 acres. Municipal records show that this parcel belongs to four immensely rich owners. The area is strategic because of its potential for urban development west of Ciudad Juárez, along the Chihuahua–New Mexico border.

The rapaciousness of the real estate industry has long been associated with Los Angeles' original urban development scheme, devised within a kind of "ecology of evil," left in the hands of investors who denude, level, and then pave the landscape, paying little attention to water, so they might better erect bulwarks and connect parcels of land, which are their "products."[10] Ultimately, these investors see the desert as nothing more than a two-sided abstraction: the intertwining of money and garbage.

In Ciudad Juárez, organized crime has come to exist side by side with "legitimate" economic power. The benefits are mutual. One serves the other. Their squabbles and pacts alternate: Politics is an electoral struggle sponsored by one party or the other. Connections between prominent Ciudad Juárez families and organized crime have been exposed in the press for years. Mexican authorities have refused to make any serious inquiries into such accusations.[11] An official document released by Wikileaks indicates that prominent businessmen hired the Zetas cartel to guard their property and protect their interests.[12] The femicide machine continues.

Ciudad Juárez has lived through the disintegration of traditional institutions as it has suffered a deepening wound. This climate of rupture and dispersion results from, among other factors, the region's centuries-old isolation. Far away from Central Mexico, and above all from Mexico City, Juárez represents a complete alienation from the larger nation. The sense of belonging to a distant axis, nearly forgotten by the center and forced to stand up for itself against the United States, is common among Ciudad Juárez residents. They disdain the idea of a nationality that ascribes to Mexico's central powers.

Within this *norteño* identity, whose roots invoke fanatical masculinity, evil tends to come only from outside the community. Especially from the south—from below, from *the* low, from the south of Chihuahua, and the south of Mexico—particularly the evil of an inequitable, sudden, and dizzying growth that began in Juárez in

1970; the difficulties arising from migratory flow; and the floating population drawn by a city that is also a nexus of bridge, wall, and garbage dump.

Natives of Ciudad Juárez attribute border problems less to local processes than "external forces" that represent the result of failed economic, political, and security strategies designed in the center of Mexico. The north of Mexico, a bulwark against harassment from the US and, at the same time, an experiment in binational integration, becomes a land of realities and of imaginary hauntings. Within this discourse, the inhabitants of Ciudad Juárez see themselves as the most *norteño* among Mexican border cities.

In Ciudad Juárez, low wages and poor quality of life result not only in real shortages, but also symbolic ones. People become dehumanized, reduced to being one more cog in an enormous production machine: the ultra-capitalist city. Integrity breaks down, not just individually, but also collectively; they mutate into fragmented beings. Society itself acquires an asocial status: its members feel disconnected from it. Conditions of continuous commotion and flux are accompanied by a feeling of rootlessness.

In the public arena, the gap between political parties and the expectations of society results in low electoral participation: Only 30 percent of registered voters actually go to the polls. As conditions experienced by the pre-citizen, pre-political, impoverished mass become more generalized, the sense of impermanence, and the lack of belonging or participation multiplies. Terror, discouragement, and rage fill the political void left by a media-controlled process. Citizens reside somewhere between survival and a transversal alternative:[13] the search for new directions in civil action.

In 2006, the Spanish artist Santiago Sierra conceived a site-specific work to be installed in Ciudad Juárez between October 2006 and March 2007. On an empty desert lot beside a US-adjacent slum, the word *submission* would be excavated, letter-by-letter, in Helvetica typeface.[14] Each letter was to be forty-nine feet long, and would be dug like a ditch, with concrete lining the walls and the floors.

Since 1974, a forty-nine acre portion of this area, which was considered to have significant real estate development potential, was taken over by settlers and schoolteachers. Since then, the settlers have battled authorities to obtain basic services and regularize the settlement. Immigrants and the poor live here. The area is a corridor for undocumented migrants, criminals, and police officers from both countries. Due to pollution from the nearby ASARCO (American Smelting and Refining Company) plant, thousands of cases of blood poisoning in children have been documented, along with acute physical malformations, anencephaly, and breathing disorders among adult residents.

The slum lies at the foot of Cristo Negro Hill, where the bodies of at least seven murdered women have been found. Sixty squatting families lay claim to the parcel of land chosen for Sierra's installation. The letter-trenches were designed to contain fuel that, when lit, would spell the word *submission* in flames. The fires would burn for thirty minutes, and a small airplane would record the event, while images shot from a crane would be broadcast live on the Internet. Black and white images would alternate on four screens, appearing for varying durations—an ultracontemporary performance.

Claiming environmental risks, the authorities prevented the event from occurring. In 2009, the Grupo México mining group purchased ASARCO, which had declared bankruptcy in 2005; a financial maneuver designed to avoid numerous lawsuits. Grupo México, Mexico's largest mining company, earned large profits from the acquisition. The plant remains inactive. It will be dismantled, and the real estate sold at auction to investors seeking to create urban development. The human costs are part of the overall profit:[15] necropolitics and its profitable amnesia.

WAR CITY/MEXICO-USA

Mexico's war on drug trafficking, sponsored by the US—the world's largest market for and consumer of drugs—began in 2006 and resulted in more than 30,000 deaths by 2011. Twenty percent of those deaths occurred in Ciudad Juárez. The war, which began as a "pilot project," has now turned the border city into an even more dangerous and desolate place than it was in the previous decade, with 116,000 abandoned dwellings, 80,000 small businesses shuttered, 10,000 orphaned children, and 200,000 families exiled.

During these five years, the Mexican army mobilized an average of 48,000 soldiers every month to combat the drug cartels, and acquired a vast arms stockpile.[1] Between 2007 and 2010, Mexico's military spending doubled, ranking fourth highest in Latin America.[2] Despite this military campaign, organized crime has grown stronger both inside and outside Mexico.

The Mexican government initiated three strategies and took additional actions in Ciudad Juárez to try to establish control of the border city. Each failure only multiplied the problems of a region ravaged by organized crime, institutional corruption, and government shortages.

In the spring of 2008, the state of Chihuahua saw the beginning of a Joint Operative, which would later be called Coordinated Operation. The army and the federal police took charge of local security, installed ten mixed-operations bases and 46 mobile checkpoints. They had 180 vehicles, 13 sets of "molecular detection" equipment to check for drugs, explosives, firearms and money, in addition to three C-130 Hercules planes and a Boeing 727/110 from the Mexican Air Force. Twenty-five hundred soldiers were deployed. The next year there were 7,000 soldiers in addition to 2,000 federal police officers.

The army and the federal police occupied different points throughout the city and practiced patrols and other tactical operations. Ciudad Juárez was so broken that its inhabitants rejected this presence: accusations of armed forces abuse have been steadily accumulating in the archives of national and international human rights organizations.[3] Later, due to US demands, the army was replaced by the federal police force. With the exception of certain privileged zones, urban life transpired within a climate of war and collective survival.

Anyone who visited Ciudad Juárez in 2010 could confirm the absolute absence of the rule of law along the border. Neither the president, the Chihuahua state government, nor Mexico's congress or political parties wanted to face the problem. Municipal authorities, state and local police, and the Mexican Army wanted to do so even less. The political diagnosis reflected a consensus: Write off Ciudad Juárez as lost.

This grave institutional perception of the city was due to the Mexican government's failed efforts to combat organized crime and the big business of drugs. But this institutional defection began long ago, ever since federal, state, and municipal authorities in Chihuahua began taking money from organized crime in exchange for judicial immunity.[4] That pact led to the erosion of institutional order. In 1993, a former federal security police commanding officer, who had until then been the boss of the Juárez cartel, was assassinated so that a drug trafficker, originally from the state of Sinaloa, could replace him. Then in 1997, he disappeared from the scene, leaving his brother in charge of a border-based criminal empire, maintained by his connections to Mexico's political and economic powers.[5] Behind this criminal mechanism lies a financial structure that creates multiple and invisible connections to the formal economy.

Despite a warrant issued for his arrest on a variety of charges since 1998—in addition to a multi-million dollar reward offered by the United States—the Juárez cartel boss has remained free and clear of harassment by the Mexican authorities for more than a decade. A resident of Ciudad Juárez,[6] he witnessed the defection of one associate, who became his number one enemy in 2004 as the head of the Sinaloa or Pacific cartel.

The key to the Juárez cartel's impunity is the strength of its network of economic and political allies. The cartel can count on this network of prominent men and women along the border, throughout the rest of Mexico, and above all, in Mexico City. The cartel also maintains strong allies north of the border.

In 2009, violence was on the rise in Ciudad Juárez. By the end of that year, the executions of 2,658 women and men had been documented as casualties of the drug war. Eighty percent of the victims were younger than 30 years old. Ciudad Juárez has the highest middle-school dropout rate in Mexico. In a city that is also home to the highest high school drop out rates and the largest percentage of 12- to 18-year-olds who neither study nor work. Their options are unemployment, drug trafficking, petty crime, suicide. The danger expands. A growing presence of Mexican drug traffickers residing in El Paso, Texas, has been reported.[7]

The official discourse on Ciudad Juárez describes only a "troubled" locale where the government fights organized crime. But for the last two decades, the Juárez cartel and its allies—prominent border individuals—have perpetrated the kidnapping, torture, rape, and murder of women; crimes of extreme deviance that began with female industrial park employees which in turn intimidated the authorities. It also served to reaffirm the cartel's exclusive dominion over this strategic nexus for smuggling drugs, arms, people, products, and merchandise, in addition to money-laundering the proceeds of these illicit activities. This is how the femicide machine began. Years later, terror returned in the form of attacks by criminal gangs on the civilian population.

Supported by gangs like *Los Aztecas* and many others, the Juárez cartel and its armed branch, *La Linea*, are waging war on the Mexican government and the Sinaloa/Pacific cartel for control of Ciudad Juárez. The presence of federal police and the army has been restricted mostly to tactical surveillance.

There is no concerted, proactive defense against organized crime in Ciudad Juárez. Consequently, what remains is a useless and brutal government operation that constantly harasses the civilian population and tramples its rights. The Mexican government refuses to wage a real fight against these privileged criminals. Instead, it prefers social welfare efforts designed to "reconstruct the fabric of society" along the border.[8] These efforts are promoted through large-scale government propaganda campaigns among the populace.

Recognizing the gravity of human rights problems in Ciudad Juárez, the United Nations proposed sending a special commission on summary executions to the city in 2009. The Mexican government refused to allow the visit.

At the beginning of 2010, a commando attack opened fire on dozens of young teenagers at a party. Sixteen died. Weeks later, another group of young people in Ciudad Juárez was attacked at another party. Seven were injured; one young man was instantly killed. The offense reproduced the first attack's method. Throughout the year, these kinds of attacks continued to be unleashed on peaceful young people enjoying themselves in private spaces.

The use of gang members and former police officers to carry out acts of intimidation and extermination against civilians serves to support the government's strategy of installing a police state, subject to military and paramilitary practices. The model for this strategy is the so-called Colombia Plan. Negotiated in 1999 between Colombia and the United States, it became the blueprint for the 2008 Merida Initiative, also known as the Merida or Mexico Plan.[9] The differences between both plans are confluent in their shared objective: the multiplication of violence.

Rule of law does not exist in Mexico, just as it is absent in Ciudad Juárez.

The Mexican government refuses to acknowledge this fact, despite a 99 percent rate of impunity from prosecution enjoyed by all criminals nationwide,[10] despite the failure of anti-drug trafficking strategies that have only worsened security and strengthened organized crime, and despite the increasing number of human rights violations committed by military and police personnel in the course of anti-drug trafficking violations.

The government denies protecting drug cartels, but it has avoided taking significant action to dismantle the financial structure of organized crime and its connections to political and economic power bases in Mexico. According to the US Department of Homeland Security, between 19 and 29 billion dollars are laundered each year in Mexico.[11] The Mexican government rejects these figures. At the same time, it admits the gravity of the problem, but refuses to fully apply the Palermo Convention Protocol to fight transnational organized crime, which Mexico joined in 2000. An estimated 78 percent of the nation's economy has been penetrated by drug trafficking.[12] The economy, just like the Mexican State, lives a drugged-up existence.

Mexican drug cartels grew stronger throughout the first decade of the twenty-first century. The leader of the Sinaloa/Pacific cartel ranks 41 in *Forbes* magazine's list of the 67 World's Most Powerful People. *Time Magazine* has included him among the world's 100 most influential people. His story is illustrative.

After seven decades of rule under the Institutional Revolutionary Party (PRI), Mexico achieved its first presidential party switch with the election of the National Action Party (PAN) in December 2000. Soon thereafter, the aforementioned criminal escaped from a maximum-security prison, setting off an unprecedented boom for Mexican drug traffickers. By then, Mexico had changed from being a thruway for hard drugs to a market, and this surge in cartel activity had unprecedented growth in the rest of Latin America and Europe, at the same time as it consolidated its US market.

The international prestige enjoyed by Mexican drug traffickers is an emblem of the government's failed war on organized crime. The government has reduced itself to making arrests and seizures.

Free to travel across the sierras of Sinaloa and Durango in the north, or in the south of Mexico and Central America, for years the leader of the Sinaloa/Pacific cartel has battled other groups, like the Zetas, over localities, territories, and routes for a market whose importance has reached global proportions: Since 2003, Mexican drug traffickers have assumed leadership in transporting drugs from South America to other parts of the world. Supremacy in Mexico is the gateway to dominance in other countries, which explains why these struggles are so fierce.

Institutional inefficiency and corruption are decisive factors in Mexico's failed war on drugs. An insoluble problem for Mexico, this war has begun to challenge the rest of the Americas and Europe. The UN Office on Drugs and Crime notes that Mexican drug traffickers now trans-port cocaine consumed in Europe—produced in Colombia, Peru, and Bolivia—displacing Colombians from drug-trafficking roles. Mexican traffickers are competing with Venezuelans to bring drugs to the continent, particularly, through West Africa.[13] An estimated 90 percent of the drugs that reach Europe arrive in this manner.

The rise of Mexican cartels worldwide involves 38 nations in Europe, Africa, and the Middle East. This has alarmed Spanish, German, and Italian authorities. A 2009 Europol report affirms that cocaine is transported from its place of origin to Venezuela, Brazil, and the Caribbean, in addition to Mexico, Costa Rica, and Panama.[14] This activity also signals the failure of other governments in the Americas.

Mexican drug traffickers excel in intercontinental drug transportation. They have now replaced Colombians as the world's largest drug distributors.[15] In 2008, more than 200 people were apprehended in the United States and Italy, after links were established between Mexico's Zetas and the Italian 'Ndrangheta mafia organization—a 55 billion dollar per year criminal enterprise. Efficient and extremely violent, the Mexican drug traffickers transport cocaine from Colombia to New York, and from there the drugs go to Italy. The us government has designated the Zetas cartel as a transnational crime organization that poses a threat to us interests.

The UN warns that drug trafficking entails more than just trafficking drugs: It spawns other criminal industries, including money laundering, kidnapping, extortion, theft, human exploitation, and the transportation of firearms, in addition to generalized violence. The situation in Latin America is alarming and presents a scenario that Europe finds troubling. As the UN Office on Drugs and Crime notes, Latin America and the Caribbean have the highest combined violent crime rates in the world. This violence—originating with drug trafficking and involving large quantities of arms and violent practices—can extend beyond those who participate in it directly,[16] a lethal infection to the established order.

The main problem lies in the way that has allowed corruption, public and private power in Mexico to strengthen the boom of drug cartels and criminal gangs. The crisis within the rule of law reveals the dark outlines of the global order—the underground economy, whose politics is violence.[17] Blood, death, threats, exploitation, weapons, unlimited profits; this is the big business created by the illegality of drugs.

Mexico exists somewhere between the memory of its past revolutions and the certainty of its current decline: a regression of the rule of law in the face of the biggest crisis in its recent history.

In 2010, Ciudad Juárez saw the murder of a female US Embassy employee in a car bomb explosion. Federal police fired on a handful of young people protesting against violence in the city. In the state of Tamaulipas, near the Gulf of Mexico, the bodies of 72 migrants from different Latin American countries were discovered on a ranch near the US border. According to an official report, they were killed by the Zetas criminal organization. A former governor was assassinated in Colima, on the Pacific coast, as was a gubernatorial candidate in Tamaulipas. Murders, decapitation, and dismemberment occurred continuously among numerous criminal groups.

The government has persevered against drug trafficking in a number of military operations that resulted in the deaths of civilians with no connection to crime. In 2010, a military operation in Tamaulipas claimed some 100 victims, both civilians and criminals, in addition to a local reporter. His death brought Mexico's murdered-journalist death toll up to 65 (since 2000), according to Mexico's National Human Rights Commission.[18] At the beginning of the twenty-first century, Mexico became the most dangerous nation in the world to be a journalist.

At the same time, Mexico's National Human Rights Commission recorded a 300 percent increase in human rights complaints against military and police personnel involved in the war on drugs since 2006. To justify its policies, the Mexican government declared: *If you see dust in the air, it's because we're cleaning house.*

Mexico's violence and security crisis demonstrates the lack of responsibility and competence of the State, the government, and the nation's ruling class. It further reveals a social rupture within a nation unable to mount an integrated defense against threats to the established order. Mexico's institutional erosion began in the

1990s, and the violence has only increased since 2000 under the PAN party administrations.

US national security policy has been a decisive factor within this crisis. The Mexican government was forced to ramp up the war on drug trafficking, not as an act of sovereignty, but as a response to demands from the Security and Prosperity Partnership of North America, established in 2005 by US, Mexican, and Canadian governments.[19] The alarmist reaction to the September 11, 2001, terrorist attacks led to the establishment of the US Northern Command in 2002,[20] and Mexico has since joined this alliance.

The Northern Command led to the Merida Initiative (2008–2010), and Mexico's war on drug trafficking evolved under its mandates: intelligence control, a hard-line weapons buildup, military, police, and paramilitary discipline. Intelligence command is now carried out by the Pentagon and other US agencies without any objection raised by Mexican authorities.[21] The precedents of this strategy within Mexico included using the army for nationwide law enforcement, and later added the navy to this operational vanguard. The objective has been the establishment of a police state, and the result has been a nationwide spike in violence throughout the country. This follows the mobilization of the greatest human and material resources for fighting criminal violence in the country's history. Mexico is less safe now than ever before.

According to the Mexican Senate, organized crime has spread to 71 percent of its national territory.[22] Not only is this force advancing, it has diversified via other criminal industries: kidnapping, extortion, theft, human trafficking and exploitation, the hijacking of trucks and trailers, and the retail sale of drugs throughout Mexico.

The arrests of drug lords or assassins, which Mexican authorities turn into a propaganda spectacle, do little to affect drug cartel criminal activities. The individuals are replaced immediately. New groups surface and begin balkanizing national territory.

The fight against organized crime has been on the Mexican political agenda for twenty-five years, but inefficiency and corruption have mapped out a path destined for failure. When the Mexican government signed the Merida Initiative with the United States, it was obliged to "strengthen" its security institutions. Unfortunately, Mexican authorities relied on fallacies when designing the war on drug trafficking.

Misjudging the situation and the methods of combat that would be needed to fight it, the Mexican government proceeded on five false premises:

1) Can be considered organized crime an agent *outside* the nation's institutions rather than something inherent to them.

2) Can be reduced the problem to a law-enforcement/criminological matter, with complex drug-trafficking and criminal industries on one side, and security agencies on the other; when in fact connivance and corrupt contact are maintained between them—a collusion that pits some groups against others for control of markets, routes, and territories.

3) The decline of police, ministerial, judicial, and correctional authority can be hidden; when in fact, this has the gravest effect: a nearly absolute (99 percent) impunity for criminals in Mexico.

4) It can ignore the fact that for the US, the problem of drug trafficking is really a geopolitical issue in which the government typically employs a double standard in order to protect its interests and national security.

5) It can ignore the fact that a war's theater of operations is always more broad than that suggested by certain localities where violence erupts, such as in Ciudad Juárez.

The State, the government, and the ruling classes refuse to change their approach as the crisis escalates to even greater levels of violence. The lie that presumes this violence results from the success of government offenses, collapsing under its own weight. Even worse—with the pretext of an already erroneous strategy, the police state becomes normalized within public and private life. The war machine rises as a regression towards the future.

Drug-trafficking corruption has been implanted in Mexico by entities charged with upholding the law and administering justice; by national intelligence agencies, militias, and police forces; by state-level governments; by the nation's political parties and judicial system; and by its banking and financial systems (B1). In Latin America, the intertwining of organized crime with national institutions in each country has flourished under the corrupting presence of drug cartels (above all, the Mexican cartels) and criminal gangs, who each day exert more influence over the continent while maintaining important connections to US and European economies.[23] The UN has issued alerts about rising demands for drugs in Africa and Latin America, whose governments lack the resources to deal with the social problem of drug addiction. Rich nations impose drug habits upon the poor while relegating them to the production and distribution of controlled substances. This exchange is doubly perverse, because it sows seeds of instability and increases the risk of criminal insurgency within those societies.

Every country proposes similar solutions based on a prohibitionist attitude towards drug use: a repressive and blameful policy based on government use of violence and weaponry. The process of installing a police state begins with the establishment of a single national police force, subject to external control by the most powerful government or international organizations. Authority is concentrated and centralized within an interior ministry. Local authority becomes vulnerable, and the integration of military forces—in Mexico's case, with the United States—is increased. Such measures are presented as "solutions," but in fact they only complicate a severe problem, with global impact.

The notion of space, region, and territory has changed with the expansion of the global economy and the growth of an information society. Borders, for example, strategic tension zones, became porous, ductile, vehicular, and fluid, largely because of migratory phenomena (B2). The war machine and the crime machine feed on borderlines, chiefly based on two factors: human trafficking or exploitation, and arms trafficking. Since September 11, the United States has considered its border with Mexico a national security priority, escalating traditional tensions between the two nations. In 2011, despite plans to erect a wall spanning the Mexican border, the US government acknowledged that it maintained effective control of only 15 percent of the border, while exercising "operative response capabilities" over the rest.[24] The "armor" seems precarious.

Unlike old-fashioned, static national borders, twenty-first century borders are liquid and flexible. This results in the interactive penetration of cultures from both sides. This new kind of border creates a *transborder*. It produces *translineal* spaces that alter the meaning and representation of identity and function within these regions. The *transborder* displays temporalities, configurations, and emergent mutations (B3). Each side of the border exchanges information and then modifies itself in relation to the other: The two sides clash, dialogue, repel and fuse, either temporarily or permanently.

Since at least the 1960s, when industrial assembly established itself and began to attract migration, these phenomena have been apparent at the Mexico/us border. Four decades later, the results of a global/local anomaly were apparent: a territory that, on the Mexican side, reflects the combined but unequal, unstable, expansive development, affecting the economy, politics, society, and culture. Ciudad Juárez shares its border with El Paso, Texas, the second-safest city in the us.[25] Such contrasts feed xenophobia on the us side of the Rio Grande. Twelve thousand illegal arms sales and entry points exist on the Mexican/us border.[26]

Consequently, many attribute the crux of the Mexican crisis to lie in the strategic exchange— drugs for guns—between the US and Mexico.

The racket has variables. Between 2009 and 2010, under the pretext of tracking illicit commerce,[27] the US Bureau of Alcohol, Tobacco, Firearms, and Explosives allowed thousands of guns to be trafficked to criminals in Mexico. Mexican demand for firearms as a result of the war on drug trafficking is a growth market for the US firearms industry;[28] this is another aspect of binational relations.

The border along the desert shared by Texas, New Mexico, and Chihuahua has the potential for institutional anomalies at best, and at worst, pure barbarism. Evidence and indications of the culture that will remain, and the microphysics of daily life, lie in the borderland's folds and creases.

A visualization of the notion of translineal space is apparent in three sites whose existence and symbolism are especially pertinent to the situation in Ciudad Juárez: the bridge, the wall, and the garbage dump. The international bridge essentially works as a valve, controlling the flow of humans seeking work in the US, drug smuggling, and the transferring of arms into Mexico. The wall is the failed container of the transborder area, and the garbage dump represents the most realized product of a sinister ecology that converts a developing nation's cities into garbage dumps or "backyards" for the developed nation it shares a border with. The narrative of geopolitical interests (B4) fully demonstrated by history.

No one wants to remember that Mexico's degradation began in the heart of its institutions. The country's drug-trafficking criminal machine is inherent in its political and economic institutions. And the us is involved. Mexico's adverse situation at the beginning of the 21st century had been gestating for some time, and is related to State agreements struck with numerous criminal groups (B5). These accords, made in exchange for money, were the origins of today's cartels. From that time forward, Mexican territory was committed to the transportation of drugs from South America. Military and police forces were corrupted, and in turn, so were the economy, politics, and society.

Mexico's support of the us government's Iran/Contra operation within Mexican territory beginning in 1981 set the precedent for these agreements. Delivering firearms to Nicaraguan anti-guerrilla forces in exchange for drugs to be sold on the us market was an operation conceived and operated by the cia. Its Mexican partner was its correlative, the Mexican Federal Security Office. The us National Security Council Directive 5412 was issued on March 15, 1954, to ensure that covert operations would be planned and conducted in a manner consistent with us foreign and military policies. The role was assigned to the Central Intelligence Agency.

This network of complicity led to two assassinations: the murder of a Mexican journalist in 1984, and one year later, the death of an American anti-narcotics agent. Both had discovered the until-then confidential connections between drug trafficking and the United States and Mexican governments.[29] This two-headed ghost hovers over Mexico's degradation, and over the US's ambiguous attitude towards the drug problem in North America and in its international relations to the south.

In recent decades, the US has sponsored or induced democratic change in the Americas, resulting in scant social improvement. Instead, poverty, marginalization, organized crime, drug trafficking, and the consequent degradation of institutions have proliferated.

For the US, control of Mexico and Central America is achieved within a context of national/regional crises that allow for the paramilitarization of these territories—achieved, in some cases, by mercenaries paid by the Pentagon. These crises spawn a boom in firearms stockpiling and intelligence or punitive operations favoring US interests. Historical accounts from around the world detail this situation in depth.[30] Drug trafficking and its attendant criminal industries serve as a pretext for the US's interventionist strategy at the dawn of the twenty-first century. In its first phase, two sub-continental points of irradiation and impact are distinguished: Mexico, for Central America, and Colombia, for South America.

In 2004, the US government reposted DEA agents stationed throughout Mexico to the state of Michoacan, on the Pacific. Corrupt government agencies had been permitting the Tijuana, Sinaloa, Gulf, and Milenio cartels to pick up drug shipments along the coast and transport them inland. The US government feared that connections between Colombian guerrillas and Mexican drug traffickers would enable terrorists from the Middle East to reach Mexico's northern border. For some time, the DEA had presumed the existence of an alliance between Al-Qaeda and Colombian guerrillas. The first action taken by Mexico's new presidential administration in 2006 was to deploy an army to Michoacan to reduce the influence of drug trafficking in that region. From time to time, the US has maintained the theory that an alliance exists between Mexican drug cartels and Al-Qaeda. Mexico has denied this possibility.[31] In 2011, the United States government insisted that an Al-Qaeda presence existed alongside the Zetas, a gang of assassins who broke with the Gulf cartel to launch its own criminal enterprise stretching all the way to Europe.

The Zetas founders are Mexican army deserters who received elite training in Mexico and the United States. Their current leader received military training at Fort Benning in Georgia and is not a fugitive from the law.

The US request to consider Mexican drug traffickers as terrorists is important not only to US geopolitics, but also to the new global State, since terrorism is the largest "de-Statifying" enemy that must be fought.[32] On its end, Mexico has proposed a legal initiative that would equate certain kinds of organized crime with the crime of terrorism.[33] This initiative reflects the construction of a common enemy: *narco-terrorism*, whose threat justifies a "state of exception" that suspends the rights of citizens and civil liberties.

The Western Hemisphere Institute for Security Cooperation—formerly the School of the Americas—has traditionally been the place where the Pentagon and US intelligence agencies integrate Latin American officers into a framework of covert operations. The objective is the imposition of an imperialist strategy: domination without direct military occupation, alternately combating risks like terrorism and radical populism.

Because of its geopolitical expectations and intelligence analyses, the United States remains alert to all activities south of the border. In 2011, a US official warned of "unprecedented levels of violence stirred up by turf wars between cartels" and "terrible crimes" occurring in the crossfire. Praising binational efforts, she proclaimed, "We need to stand by Mexico until the end of this war."[34] Less explicitly stated—and therefore more clearly read—was that the United States *demanded* this war from the Mexican government.

Her statements were preceded by the declaration of another US official that a sort of "insurgency," led by drug trafficking cartels, existed in Mexico. This insurgency "could potentially take over the government" and would demand a US military response. Mexico denied this threat, and the US government promptly insisted that the Mexican situation constituted a permanent risk to US national security. The director of US intelligence declared that Mexico's military and police forces were spread too thin, and incapable of combating narco-terrorism. The intensity of these declarations was meaningful. The US exerts two lines of discourse and practice, the formal and informal (in fact: covert or special activities) in its conduct of bilateral relations, using protocol to make its internal logic explicit. For public purposes, the discourse acts as a geopolitical blockade. Meanwhile, different US agencies pursue their own agendas.

Since 1959, a great many of the United States' wars have been induced and waged in what is described as a response to "enemy aggression": a profound deceit and manipulation of events that often involves a global connection to drugs (B6). The CIA has been involved with Mexico throughout its long history of worldwide operations. These operations are historically aimed at disrupting the internal stability of other nations in ways that will be favorable to immediate or future US interests: exerting dominance or influence, exploiting or accumulating natural resources. Petroleum, for example, is abundant in the Gulf of Mexico, yet unlike the US petroleum industry, Mexico lacks the technology to take advantage of its best deposits. Another example is uranium; there are more than fifty uranium deposits in Chihuahua.

The US has demanded that Mexico open a new front in the war on drug trafficking along its border with Guatemala. Conflicts will increase in this organized-crime dominated area.[35] But despite resistance to this operation by the Mexican government, a new phase of the Merida Initiative— repositioning Mexico's role as monitor of its southern border with Central America—is foreseeable.[36] The region's weakness demands Mexican support. Meanwhile, the US has expanded its role in the battle against Mexican drug cartels by 400 percent.

Connections between the CIA and Mexican drug traffickers are never deeply investigated by either government. In 2007, a private plane used by the

CIA for clandestine flights with suspected terrorists in it crashed in southeast Mexico. The plane was carrying nearly three tons of Colombian cocaine belonging to the Sinaloa/Pacific cartel.[37] The plane was purchased in the US for $2 million with cash at a currency-exchange business later raided by Mexican authorities. Investigations revealed that drug-traffickers had purchased at least twelve additional planes in this fashion. Nothing else was revealed. During the 1980s, the CIA protected principal Mexican drug traffickers, the agency itself bought and sold cocaine in the United States.[38] The story, plot, and protagonists repeat across decades; the only things that change are the names. The spy machine operates cyclically.

The Bi-national Intelligence Office is in a centrally located building in Mexico City where government functionaries, Pentagon, CIA and FBI agents, and agents from the Department of Justice, Homeland Security, and the US Treasury cohabitate.[39] The Pentagon operates through the Military Intelligence Agency, the National Geospace Intelligence Office, and the National Security Agency. The Department of Justice also has three agencies: the FBI, the DEA, and the Bureau of Alcohol, Tobacco, Firearms, and Explosives. There's also Homeland Security, along with the Coast Guard Intelligence Agency, the Customs and Immigration Enforcement Office; the

Treasury Department brings in agents from the Office of Terrorism and Financial Intelligence. The Bi-national Intelligence Office also has facilities in Tijuana and Ciudad Juárez.

The use of US mercenaries in Mexico to fight the war on drug trafficking is well documented, but both the Mexican and US governments refuse to acknowledge this.[40] All is fair in war. And more so if the war is ordered from abroad. A variety of ultra-contemporary war methods are deployed.

The public face shown by the US towards Mexican drug trafficking has evolved over the years in the following manner:

a) A historical phase of tolerance (1920–1969).
b) Prohibitionist tolerance (1969–1985).
c) Punitive prohibition (1985–1999).
d) Binational cooperation and US certification of Mexico's war on drug trafficking (1989–2002).

Between 2002 and 2006, the drug trafficking problem became shared national emergencies. Hence, Mexico's big war on trafficking in 2006 was based on US national security policy.

A recent US judicial procedure revealed that the DEA and FBI have made recent efforts to manipulate Mexican drug traffickers in the Sinaloa cartel, as they have done in the past with other groups.[41] The US government prefers to turn a blind eye to the pragmatic aspects of these operations.

A Mexican security expert has revealed that armed US military or paramilitary forces have carried out numerous actions against Mexican criminals in the war on drug trafficking. This contradicts the official version of the story that the Mexican government has reported. All's fair in war; even more so, in wars ordered from abroad.

The problem of drug trafficking and violence cannot be reduced to a myth: the old-fashioned struggle between cops and robbers. Drug trafficking concerns the economy, politics, society, and culture. Above all, it reflects the grave institutional crisis in Latin American nations. The urgency of the problem plays out between the search for a democratic future, the gravitational pull of the global economy, and the weight of inertia and historic inequalities. Inefficiency, ineptitude, and corruption have prospered between these cracks. An economic scheme has been implanted wherein a privileged few benefit from the business of illegality and its lacerating dangers: impunity for violent and criminal activity, the fragmentation of law enforcement and justice administration.

The devastating impact of drug trafficking and the violence it imposes upon Mexican culture is far from being merely a media phenomenon, as the "magic bullet theory" might indicate (whereby media have the capacity to mold public opinion and focus on a single point of view). The prodigal business of illegality is one of Latin America's greatest threats, since it sustains itself via economic and political powers that receive enormous benefits. Governments fight, or pretend to fight organized crime, but at the same time their bureaucracies and police and armed forces open themselves up to corruption. Words and deeds are at odds within this hypocritical discourse of manipulation.

If Latin America's modernization during the past twenty-five years has yielded anything, it is the ineptitude of its ruling classes in handling the asymmetry between democratic norms, poverty, and inequality. Power transitioned through more or less overseen elections, establishing bases of continuous development. In turn, oligarchy, monopoly, and greedy corporations, contrary to any egalitarian principles, prevail.

A 2008 UN report highlighted Latin American nations' vulnerability to crime, and drug trafficking in particular, since it "is most responsible in terms of collective action."[42] Colombia, Peru, and Bolivia produce a thousand tons of cocaine annually, reaching at least ten million US and European consumers via other Latin American nations—"almost every nation in the hemisphere is affected." Cocaine production has increased, along with seizures in Venezuela, Trinidad and Tobago, Panama and Costa

Rica. This is due to the fact that, facing numerous difficulties, Colombian drug dealers are forced to extend their activities to other regions.

Increased cocaine consumption in Europe has multiplied drug trafficking through West Africa, a new flow that affects Venezuela and nations in the southern Caribbean. Even though cocaine consumption has declined in the US, it is still the world's largest market. Regarding heroin, the hemisphere satisfies international demand, with Mexico and Colombia dealing to more than a million addicts. At the same time, consuming cannabis is universal, and every country provides its own national product, although Paraguay, Colombia, and Jamaica export this drug to other countries in the region.

The report notes that initially, methamphetamine production for domestic consumption was greater in the US than in other countries. This supply has spread to Mexico and from there, further south. The UN Office on Drugs and Crime warns that drug trafficking impacts other types of criminal activity, including insurgencies, as exemplified by Colombia and recently, Mexico. In Latin America, drug trafficking is inseparable from the surge in violence. If drug trafficking seems to be everywhere, it is because societies everywhere recognize that their expansive centers lie precisely in their deceitful institutions. Mexico is currently the most visible example on the world stage, even though its government denies the gravity of the problem.

According to the report, this pervasive context explains the boom in criminal gangs like the Central American *Maras* and their culture of crime affirmation. Money laundering and corruption become additional factors that erode economies and governments within this "hemispheric problem." Notably, marijuana consumption has increased across Latin America, particularly in Argentina, Uruguay, Paraguay, Peru, Venezuela, Jamaica, the Dominican Republic, Honduras, and Mexico. The report concludes that "drug trafficking is one of the many sources of crime the region faces but, of course, it is the largest and perhaps most difficult problem [since] there is no nation in Latin America that isn't affected by drug trafficking." While drug-related violence can be diffuse in the large cities of consumer nations, it often concentrates at bottlenecks—zones and corridors where trafficking occurs, like Ciudad Juárez. This violence is far from being a social conflict like any other. It is a cyclical effect: "Drug trafficking undermines the rule of law, and weakness in the rule of law facilitates drug trafficking." Minimizing the problem now and in the future only implies a path of lies and defection. It facilitates the perpetuity of the war machine and the crime machine, along with their age-old interconnections.

4

FEMICIDE MACHINE

The phenomenon of female homicides in Ciudad Juárez began to be denounced in 1993. There is evidence these crimes began years before. Why were they murdered? For the pleasure of killing women who were poor and defenseless.

How many victims have there been? Of the 400 women and girls killed for various reasons from 1993 to the present, at least 100 murders were commited in tandem with extreme sexual violence. The lack of reliable information from the authorities is part of the problem.

Who killed them? Drug traffickers, complicit with individuals who enjoy political and economic power.

Where and how did the events take place? The victims were abducted from the streets of Ciudad Juárez and taken by force into safe houses where they were raped, tortured, and murdered at stag parties or orgies.

The victims' bodies were dumped into the desert like garbage, tossed onto streets, on corners and vacant lots in the city's urban and suburban zones, and in the outskirts of the city. In many cases the victims' clothes and identification cards were interchanged in a kind of perverse game. Authorities refused to investigate the cases in depth. These events imply a misogynistic furor that escalated from an isolated crime to a collective ravaging; especially in terms of the "copycat effect," in which imitators stalk victims and replicate the femicide machine's efficiency. Impunity is the murderers' greatest stimulant.

These are the conclusions of numerous experts in Mexico and abroad, who launched investigations on this phenomenon, independently of the Mexican government's own investigations. Neither the Mexican state nor its government has confronted the problem during its various stages in a manner congruent with their official responsibilities. There is no mystery about these murders beyond the failure of Mexican authorities to undertake an in-depth investigation of these crimes. A number of politicians and government officials have promised to carry out investigations, and they have even publicly vowed to request help from the United States to resolve the problem. None of these promises have been kept. The facts point to a situation that extends beyond Mexico's borders.

A report by a UN expert panel visiting the border in the fall of 2003 noted: "A total of 328 women have been murdered in Ciudad Juárez during the 1993–2003 period. Of this total number, 86 aggravated homicides have been perpetrated involving sexual violence."[1] Another academic study raised the figure to 144 victims in 2004.[2] Within this universe of cases, some would be what many criminologists identify as serial murders.

The UN's report lamented "the relative incapacity of the State to adequately solve these cases." The true cause of such ineptitude resides in the efficacy of the femicide machine, whose functioning has evolved over time, incorporating judicial and political systems, to such an extent that Mexican authorities have sidetracked or blocked the investigations. This performance goes beyond the mere incompetence or negligence which some have cited to justify their own actions. Authorities have continually discredited those who oppose their official version of the truth: The crimes, they insist, are merely a product of domestic violence, or, more recently, the war on drug trafficking. They seek to discount the systematic and peculiar violence against women, a violence wherein organized crime and Juárez's political and economic powers converge.

An FBI source affirmed: "Who's behind the murders? At least one or more serial killers, a couple of drug dealers, two violent and sadistic gangs and a group of powerful men."[3] Mexican government intelligence officials have also sustained this view. Mexican authorities and their spokespeople have tried to minimize the events in Ciudad Juárez, seeking to shift public attention toward generalized misogynist violence throughout Mexico, ultimately confronting neither problem.

The Mexican government declares that most of the murders of women in Ciudad Juárez have been solved. In Mexico, as long as the authorities accuse someone—with or without proof—a case is deemed "solved."

Organizations for the families of victims argue that nothing has been resolved.

In 2005, a little girl was kidnapped on a street near her house. Her body was found, days later, inside a plastic container filled with cement. She had been assaulted and sexually mutilated. She was seven years old. Another girl suffered a sexual assault in her house and was killed by asphyxiation. Her house was burned down. The victim was ten. Thirty-six victims were reported that year, attacked in various circumstances.

According to press documentation and official data, 22 murders against women were committed in 2006, and at least 14 in the course of 2007.

In 2008, the body of a twenty-year-old woman was found in Ciudad Juárez. She had suffered three stab wounds to the neck and eight more to the back. She had been living in the border town for a very short time. She was a student, and employed in a store. On the night of the murder, she came home from a party alone, and was murdered. Her family was out of town. She suffered sexual abuse. That year, the murders of at least 87 women were reported, attributed to various causes; 24 of them involved sexual abuse and extreme violence.

In 2009, there were 164 murders of women in Ciudad Juárez and 306 similar murders in 2010. They died from strangulation, stabbing, and gunshots. The brutality on their bodies was habitual. The rise of this type of violence coincides with the war on drugs and a boom in border insecurity.

Some of the accomplices within this fabric of unpunished crime remain in the public arena: Politicians, government employees, judges and police officers remain safe from questioning. Others, whose work is unsuitable to the power interests involved, have been threatened or murdered as authorities continue to fabricate culprits instead of commissioning in-depth investigations.

The Office of the Mexican Attorney General, the agency that administrates federal justice, has refused to undertake an investigation into the murders of women in Ciudad Juárez. The Attorney

General's office deems these crimes subject to state jurisdiction because of their "local nature," stemming from domestic violence or "crimes of passion." Its only involvement has been through an agreement to provide technical and legal assistance to local authorities. The Attorney General's office insists that these crimes fall within state jurisdiction despite the real and feigned incompetence Chihuahua has demonstrated—the state of Chihuahua is notorious for the condemnation it has received from both national and international entities—and despite the fact that there is evidence that these murders are connected to federal crimes.

Numerous circumstances reveal the responsibility taken by Mexican authorities:

• In 1998, Mexico's National Commission on Human Rights issued Recommendation 44/98, which demanded that police and authorities be investigated for the murders of women in Ciudad Juárez. Authorities refused to do so. In 2003, the Commission issued a report condemning the federal government's oversight before the problem.

• *The Report from the UN International Commission of Experts, Office of Drugs and Crime*, regarding their Mission in Ciudad Juárez, Chihuahua, Mexico, November 2003 condemned Mexican authorities for their inefficient action in the case of the murders of women in Juárez.

• The "resolution" of cases the government presumes is based on a bureaucratic argument that considers cases assigned to judges to be "solved," even if these cases lack evidence to support their rulings, as was demonstrated by the previously mentioned international commission of experts.

• Mexican authorities have propagated presumptions and rumors about the murdered women in Ciudad Juárez that confuse public opinion, and have caused pain and suffering to the victims and their families.

• The data used by authorities to confront the problem of the femicide machine was rejected in 2009 by the Inter-American Human Rights Commission's International Penal Court.

• The federal government's lack of interest in solving the murders of women in Ciudad Juárez reveals a premeditated policy at odds with institutional responsibilities. In fact, the government has undertaken a series of substitutive actions that avoid the administration of justice, law enforcement, and penalization.

A substitutive act is defined as one that, in the course of governance, is undertaken to manage a problem before attempting to resolve it. This reduction of policy to the administration/bureaucracy directly relies on procedural or legal resources that would permit the management and control of situations that are characterized, in a founded or unfounded manner, as "risks to governability." As such, they imply discretionary acts or acts of an a-legal nature.[4] The extent of these substitutive acts impacts government structure, its functions and policies, as well as the media environment both in and out of the country.

The result is that in the name of the law, the rule of law is made vulnerable and justice is obstructed. A parallel order.

Five substitutive acts have been enacted on behalf of the Mexican government in response to the murders of women in Ciudad Juárez:

a) The opening of a joint prosecutor's office between the government of Chihuahua and the federal government in 2003.

b) The announcement of a 40-Point Integrated Plan to combat violence in Ciudad Juárez.

c) The appointment of a Commission on Social Welfare and Public Relations, whose stated purpose was to try to "reconstruct the fabric of society along the border."

d) The creation, in 2004, of a Special Prosecutor's office within the Mexican

Attorney General's Office, charged with exclusively examining those crimes that may have been committed by police and state/local authorities while investigating the murders of women in Ciudad Juárez. In 2005, additional human and material resources were provided without altering the primary objective of merely "assisting" local state authorities.

The four actions described above were insufficient and contradictory. Consequently, they produced limited results. The actions were limited to records review and statistics certification; establishing a genetic databank and identifying a number of bodies; tracking down certain women who had been reported missing, and "supporting" the families of victims with hush money. Case investigations were ruled out.

The government's fifth substitutive act regarding Ciudad Juárez dismisses or discredits anyone who questions its official versions of the crimes, or government policy.

Besides suffering from social arrogance and gender hatred, the victims of the femicide machine in Ciudad Juárez have been raped, a crime that the International Criminal Court finds equivalent to torture. The Mexican government, which presumably complies with international rulings in such matters, has chosen a growing indifference as its policy.

The particularity of the femicide machine in Ciudad Juárez exceeds common criminality and rationalizations of government ineptitude. Arguments that these crimes can be attributed to either factor avoid government responsibility, and have been a foundation for both its propaganda discourse and its substitutive actions. They have also been used as an ideological/political stance for activists, officials, and certain civil groups close to the government.

The urgent need to comprehend the femicide machine has led some academics to pluralize the concept, and speak of Ciudad Juárez's femicides as something more than gender crimes. The femicides have been referred to as "corporate crimes," and more specifically, as "second-State or parallel-State crimes; the word 'corporation' here is used to describe the network or group that administers a parallel-State's resources, rights and duties—a network or group that is firmly established in the region, with tentacles into the nation's upper levels of hierarchy."[5]

There is an evident displacement of the criminal with the political within this idea. It began as a denunciation, resulting in the construction of a discourse which deviates from the norm. The term "femicide"[6] was first applied in 1997 to

describe the victims of Ciudad Juárez. From the
end of the 1990s to the present, the word "femicide" has become a verbal compound, assumed
and adapted by Mexican society as *feminicidio*
("feminicide"). Thus, the term was used interna-
tionally;[7] at times inserted into an almost obligatory
synonymy: Femicide equals the murder of women
in Ciudad Juárez.

Confronting the problem involves engaging
with at least two levels of political perspective:
first, a search for justice and truth for these victims
of male barbarity that has been normalized by
institutions, and at the same time challenging the
official position that denies the facts of these
crimes; second, a confrontation between the
present and the past: an insistence on memory, in
light of official disdain and oblivion.

In 2004, an academic group of experts in violence against women proposed an alternative plan
to Mexican authorities in order to confront the
Ciudad Juárez problem. The plan sought to shed
light on the murders by establishing a unique
investigative structure that would examine each
and every case. There would be justice for the
victims; damages suffered by family members
would be repaired. A greater awareness of crimes
committed along the border would be fostered.
The plan proposed legal reforms, as well as a
number of political and administrative measures

that would be taken on federal, state, and local levels. The initiative was presented to the executive and legislative branches of the government, among other entities.[8] Authorities refused to put the initiative into practice.

In Mexico, a General Law on Women's Access to a Violence Free Life has been passed, based on the notion of "feminicide violence."[9] In reality, the law has had little impact, due to lack of enforcement at different governmental levels.[10] It has been demonstrated that additional laws and more severe punishment have never been the ideal way to reduce crime. Not even a perfect law will remedy violence against women. The flaw lies in the human factor, and in laws that are not enforced, or in legal methods.

The murders of women in Ciudad Juárez have generated at least four major lines of contradicting discourse and narrative that converge in public life:

a) The official version, which melds information with counter-informative manipulations and propaganda about the cases.

b) The journalistic narrative, in which the official version and at times, a critical examination or a denunciation of its facts, are confluent.

c) Reports from academic and international organizations about the violent occurrences.

d) The cultural narrative, constructed by literature, film, music, art, and the theater. This narrative seeks to reinvent reality or defend historical truth based on reportage, first-person stories, fiction, or beliefs held by the community; word-of-mouth information and emerging expressions that offer a wealth of content.

The diversity of these discourses and narratives between sectors reflects the ongoing conflict between their respective bases and aims.

These discourses and narratives are expressed not only in traditional institutions—judicial and political forums, academia, the publishing industry, etc.—but also within what is known as media space, occupied by press, radio, and television. They also proliferate in transmedia and cyberspace: the internet, new technologies and platforms, and social networks.

Through these communicative processes, the murders of women in Ciudad Juárez have achieved cyber-event status, in which world vision is expanded by moving beyond the restricted focus of the news item or the media event. "It originates in the dialectical interrelationship between phenomenological reality, media space, and cyberspace."[11] In the new reception field that includes the mediatic and the transmediatic, transversal tactics for understanding and resisting institutional "truths" are configured.

The attention paid to the murders of women in Ciudad Juárez, both in and outside of Mexico, has provoked denial from the Mexican government. This attitude reflects the discourse of oligarchy in Ciudad Juárez, which rejects or disqualifies a demand for justice surrounding these crimes as a "for-profit industry." Authorities and the ruling classes bemoan the loss of prestige that murdered or disappeared women bring. Their rejection is a concerted action.

Spokespeople for the Juárez oligarchy persist in denying that the murders of women constitute a problem. They rely on official statistics, devoid of credibility, or reinterpretations of journalistic sources. They allege that many men are murdered in the city as well—failing to recognize, or under-estimating misogynist aggression. They claim that the problem originates from outsiders, divulging a dark legend about the pulchritude of a hard-working locality. They blame the families of victims, feminist groups, journalists, and academics. They call the situation a "black legend," a "myth," "fiction," "exaggeration," or "fantasy." Numerous national and international experts and organiza-tions attest to the contrary. In the face of this obstinacy, a criterion persists: The denial of exter-mination is part of the extermination.

In 2009, the Inter-American Commission on Human Rights condemned the Mexican government for its inefficiency and negligence based on the cases of three of the eight murdered women found in a cotton field in 2001. Their report pointed out a lack of violence prevention against women, the inexistence of proper investigations, and the lack of guaranteed access to the judicial system for women.

The commission also condemned the failure of public prosecutors, commissions and respective Mexican government programs, and emphasized the human rights violations committed against the families of victims, particularly mothers. They noted a lack of credibility in the institutional data.[12] The Mexican government failed to respond to the hemisphere's highest court sentence within the allotted response time. In this way, the government achieved its purpose to render the victims invisible. They were deprived of their human rights just as they were previously deprived of their public, political, and civil rights. In crisis, the State withdraws, erasing the crimes from memory. The femicide machine's supremacy imposes itself.

The authorities refuse to accept responsibility for the murdered and missing women. They extend the annihilation and invisibility of victims to those who defend them, establishing their inexistence by ignoring their efforts and pursuing other priorities. The femicide machine refines its applications: It specializes in murdering or harassing those who defend human rights, in addition to the victims and their families. They are assaulted in the street or at home. They are threatened. Their goods and properties are damaged. Their families are harassed. Seventeen human rights activists and defenders have been murdered in Chihuahua since 2009.

In 2010, the mother of a young female victim of misogynist violence was killed by a hired assassin at the entrance of the Chihuahua state capitol. Due process had left the murderer at large, and the victim's mother had gone there to demand justice. No authority bothered to respond to her complaint—not the public prosecutor, the governor, the judges, or the president of Mexico, whom she'd petitioned unsuccessfully for a hearing to explain her unheard plight. Mexico stopped being what it believed itself to be a long time ago: a nation ruled by law under a specific nation-state pact. The murder in question remains unpunished.

Mexican institutions are an amorphous entity, connected less and less to reality. The government survives on propaganda and lies in the face of civil demands, taking refuge behind a supposed respect for Chihuahua's state sovereignty to avoid intervening in the case of Ciudad Juárez's murdered women.

With this perfunctory excuse, the federal government eludes its implicit responsibilities.

The rotten state of Mexican institutions is not merely a turn of rhetoric.

To putrefy is to corrupt, to effect a radical alteration of matter. This transition to another condition—in this case, degradation—demonstrates the defection of Mexico's ruling classes and its spokespeople, who now occupy the space that once belonged to the rule of law. The result is a bifurcated reality: Institutions float in a self-referential vacuum, while society follows the inertia of its own erosion. According to records from the *Nuestras Hijas de Regreso a Casa* (Bring Our Daughters Home) citizen activist group, disappearances have increased by 400 percent in Ciudad Juárez from 2008 until the present.

Amid such extremes, a collective amnesia is imposed and pervades. This amnesia is further extended through the cyclical business of elections. The past is forgotten with each new administration, succeeding only in reproducing the anomalies of their immediate predecessors.

The femicide machine also produces the disappearance of women in Ciudad Juárez and other locations in the state of Chihuahua. The authorities' statistics regarding these disappearances are as inconsistent as those concerning the murder victims. Some speak of hundreds of cases, others only of dozens.[13] Missing person ads, in search of the disappeared, are part of the urban landscape along the border.

Posted signs and flyers cry out for those who have vanished, offering a metaphor for a volatile, nomadic, and difficult urban life that has since become global. People disappear on their way into cities, on highways, in slums, garbage dumps, vacant lots, street corners, one-room rooftop apartments, in red light districts, and at the recreation centers where young people meet, or on downtown streets and the bridges that join countries.

In Ciudad Juárez, these posters and flyers spring up on poles, walls, and shop windows. A few days later they are covered by others, which will in turn be replaced by still more, in a haunting montage of faces, data, marks, and signals. *Attention. Missing. Any information is appreciated.* The clarity of bodies in blurry portraits and instant novels.

For the families of victims, the history of disappearance and eventual death is met in each case by a routine of insensitivity on the part of the authorities. Despite immediate denunciations, the authorities refuse to act—just following the rules—or they cause harm to the families in their proceedings. Often, they suggest that the disappeared person led a double life, that she was engaged in prostitution, fond of partying, or had just run away or left with a friend. In the face of these disappearances, they see nothing but family conflicts or love affairs on the run. This contempt both covers up and fosters crime, casually precondemning the victims. Such ineptitude and fraud work to ensure the invisibility of the victims. And there are signs of something worse: In Ciudad Juárez, murderers destroy the corpses of victims in their entirety. Without a body, there is no crime.

The femicide machine operates through an ultracontemporary criminal power, enjoying resources, firearms, SUVs and ATVs, safe houses, logistics, hi-tech communications devices, spy networks, and police complicity. At the same time, pre-modern beliefs are incorporated into the machine's structure: hierarchical discipline centered around faith, based on loyalty and silence, initiation rites for membership in the group or fraternity.

Atop *Cerro Bola*, overlooking Ciudad Juárez on the border of El Paso, a triangle formed by stones nearly ten feet long on each side was discovered in the year 2000. Near there, not long before, the bodies of at least two murdered women bearing signs of strangulation, sexual abuse, and torture were discovered.

The triangle was formed, along with larger rocks at four points, by 46 stones on each side

(46 x 3 = 138; 1 + 3 + 8 = 12; 1 + 2 = 3). Its base featured a nearly foot-wide opening. The apex faced south, and the opening at the base pointed north, to the United States. The rocks were an offering shaped like a heart, simultaneously parodying the Holy Trinity. The recurrence of threes and fours (3 x 4 = 12) seems to be a temporal allusion of the number 12—12 months? 12 years? About 500 paces were measured between the stones and where the two victims were found. Inside the triangle, the land had been cleared of vegetation, and the remains of a bonfire were found to one side of the triangle.

In 1995, the semi-nude body of a murdered young woman was found on the outskirts of Ciudad Juárez. Symbolic of other murders, it had been discarded in an abandoned area amid shrubs and trash. Judicial records indicate that the body was found "lying face down, her head oriented to the north, the right arm bent beneath the abdomen and the left bent somewhat lengthwise; her legs spread." Death by strangulation was confirmed, and according to the forensics exam, it occurred at the same instant as the rapist's orgasm. Despite the decomposition of the remains, a "triangular cut wound" was observed "in the coccyx region, extending to the inner part of both gluteal regions, and the dilated anus." The criminal's signature.

During the twelve years between 1989 and 2001, dozens of girls in Chihuahua suffered sex-related murders. The most aggressive kind of criminal arrogance converged on their bodies. In some cases, similar wounds were tattooed on the sacrificed bodies in rituals of masculine affirmation—a dark warning that instigated an outbreak of copycat serial murders, abuses, and acts of violence against women and girls.

Cormac McCarthy describes the border between the United States and Ciudad Juárez as a space where "the probability of the actual is absolute."[14] The spilled blood that fertilizes the desert and mountains survives there.

The current crisis in Mexico reflects the high cost of indifference and complicity with respect to institutional decline. At one point, every murder victim in Ciudad Juárez sent out a warning cry that was either ignored or minimized by the state and Mexican government. A visceral cry in the desert. Symbolic perceptions of the desert held in relation to the murdered women depict a hostile space, lacking water and subject to extreme temperatures—a refuge for libertinism. A place opposed to culture, civilized values and urban identity.

Artist Boris Viskin's painting *Juárez* (2005) establishes a distance from the real, recasting it as a metaphysical reflection: The immensity of the desert/garbage dump absorbs the mangled body of a victim in a suburban trash heap. What might be metaphorical play acquires an urgent materiality, reflecting the banality of evil that turns a person into something less than a number—a dispossession close to absolute nothingness, a disposable piece, a preprogrammed, serial wastage. To leave a raped, abused, half-naked woman's body in a garbage dump is to resignify the body within indifference and abjection.[15] The act suppresses the distance between objects and humans, and calls out for savage disorder, a tumultuous mix of substances, forces, and inverted signs. Through it, the victim is reminded of her restricted status in domestic and industrial spheres; within the administration of dirt. Her identity is predestined not to exist. Or it is a utilitarian, replaceable existence that transcends individualism.

In 2010, the US-based cosmetics company MAC introduced a new line inspired by the murdered women of Ciudad Juárez. Created by the female designers of Rodarte, the post-Goth collection previewed in New York during Mercedes Benz Fashion Week. In a candlelit, black-light ambience, models sported lace, necklaces, and Victorian-era "poor white trash" looks, wearing makeup that heightened the cadaverous pallor of their faces. Their eyes were exaggeratedly lined in dark brown shadow, "evoking the desert," replacing the typical black that aficionados of Goth style have been using for decades. In "compensation" for this absurdity, the firm and its designers agreed to donate $100,000 to civil society organizations along the Mexican border. Like so many other personalities and phenomena, Ciudad Juárez's femicide machine reached the world of fashion.

Globalized culture is characterized by its combination of fashion, show business, advertising, news, sports, design, art, and brands. Its contents are a highly fluid substance: a substance that exchanges, overlaps, and inverts the autonomy that those dimensions and disciplines once maintained. Sport, for example, has achieved the status of art within ultramodernity, just as design has replaced politics in many communicative acts.

Appearances and perceptions have displaced mechanisms of the past that once offered meaning within a collective coexistence. The result is a banalization of reality; a process of appropriations, displacements, and symbolizations derived by extracting reality from facts and turning those facts, now relieved of their weight and context, into simple data or signs that become part of commercial creativity's available stock. Friedrich von Hayek foresaw this—the market prizes the scarce—to which the following would have to be added: The market prizes the scarce in constant degradation, since creative entropy is consubstantial with consumer habits.

In addition to being unimaginative, the use of the Ciudad Juárez femicide machine to sell cosmetics is an act of commercial stupidity. The drama of the victims of misogynist murders, the suffering of their families and friends, becomes the target of inappropriate sarcasm, an abuse and profit as cruel as those of the murderers. In this way, MAC joins the drug traffickers, the economically and politically powerful, and the authorities that have protected them throughout the years. Impunity in Ciudad Juárez rises to a whole new level in this undertaking: a line of cosmetics. It is tantamount to the deceit practiced by the corrupt authorities and their spokespeople, who insist that a femicide machine never *existed* in Ciudad Juárez. Facts that contradict official misinformation.

The marketing of makeup inspired by the drama along the US/Mexico border reflects that global culture has arrived at an incredible degree of amnesia and indifference. Scandal is also primordial. Global culture's banality is a sister to those who wish to deny the problem of the murders of women in Ciudad Juárez. But no makeup or amnesia is possible when confronted by barbarism, cruelty, and banalization.

Some time ago, the Mexican state lost its domination of violence to onslaughts from drug trafficking. Criminal impunity is absolute in Mexico. Insecurity grows day by day. The theater of military and police operations surpasses the lines of fire drawn in cities and border locales like Ciudad Juárez.

The crisis of Mexico's nation-state pact began with the decadence of a post-revolutionary model sustained during the twentieth century for more than seven decades as part of an authoritarian presidency and one-party rule. The global forces of ultraliberalism, market ideology, neo-Fordist or globalized economy, and the rise of information societies, arrived at the same moment that Mexico was trying to establish bases for democracy.

The inertias of old regimes, the political subculture of authoritarianism and large-scale oligarchic interests imposed a so-called transition to democracy that culminated in the current disaster: a nation caught in an integral crisis. The other side of this "transition" exposed links between political/economic power and drug trafficking, and its consubstantial existence alongside institutions. Simultaneously, the underground economy became, on a global level, a hidden instrument within the market.

Mexico's current crisis began with government reform movements and the imposition of a free-trade agreement with the United States and Canada. These reforms and agreements were complemented by the ruling technocracy's submission to metropolitan directives. Those who had advocated reforms and free-trade agreements protest that their failure to deliver development and prosperity lies in a lack of continuity. It becomes increasingly clear that there was a political, more than an economic, motivation that led Mexico to enter this pact. The results are obvious for all to see: Mexico's integration with North America has weakened Mexico's institutions and the entire country. Violence has escalated in Mexico since 1994. Attempting to fight it, the Mexican government instituted a 2008 constitutional reform pertaining to criminal justice and public security that has been highly criticized for being an attack individual and human rights.

Mexico's reaffirmation as a mid-level economic power was accompanied by more inequality, a higher wealth concentration and a greater number of people immersed in extreme poverty, not to mention the impoverishment of the middle class.

The first years of the twenty-first century offer a picture of the contrasts, disarticulations, deficiencies, and degradations within the nation. The Mexico of the previous century has been transformed, little by little, into the post-Mexican nation. The years 2000–2010 were economically lost, and a good deal of Mexico's labor force—more than ten million people—had to leave to find work: the other "illegal" merchandise entering us territory, in addition to drugs. The war machine, crime machine, and femicide machine arose and were imposed in this context. A certainty devoid of optimism or pessimism: It is simply the observation of a negative inertia that systemically grows and expands. Given this situation, two possible futures emerge: the evolution of a new, unforeseen model of organization, or the further devolution into a state with no functional order at all.

Epilogue

INSTRUCTIONS FOR TAKING
TEXTUAL PHOTOGRAPHS

Photographic mise-en-scène:

Ale's last day with us: she woke up at six AM and started getting ready to go to work.

Then she left me in charge of the kids, she slept on the ground floor of the house, and she asked me for bus money. She took money from my purse and went to the factory.

She wanted to take computer training courses and become a journalist.

Lilia Alejandra was seventeen and had two small children.

You'd see her with her babies and she looked like a little girl playing with her dolls.

She was very disappointed with her boyfriend, so she preferred to live with us.

We talked. That's when I asked her to look for a job, and study at the same time. She had to be someone in life.

She agreed.

She settled in well at work. Since she was pretty, they used her as a model to pose next to the products the factory produced. They took her picture a lot.

Since then I've wondered if they gave those pictures to the kidnappers and that's why they chose her.

Ale's boyfriend kept bothering her to get back with him, he'd come looking for her at home and he waited for her outside work. He harassed her, pressured her.

That's why every day I would go pick her up at the factory. She got off at seven.

The day she disappeared, I couldn't pick her up because I was taking a sex-ed course.

Imagine how many times I've dreamt and thought about the fact that Ale would be alive if I hadn't been absent that afternoon.

Here, one mistake is a life sentence.

She disappeared on February 14, Valentine's Day, when she left her job at the *maquiladora*.

They found her dead seven days later, in a vacant lot across from the Plaza Juárez shopping center, a busy area.

During the week that Ale went missing, we looked for her at the Red Cross, at the clinics. We printed a thousand flyers.

I didn't want to accept that they'd taken her.

I wondered if she'd had an accident or if she'd run away from home, but then I'd think: Ale isn't like that, she'd have said something. She was a very obedient girl. Sometimes she fought with her sister, but that always happens between brothers and sisters.

We went to file a missing person's report, which they reluctantly took. They ignored us until we insisted. Even then that didn't get us very far.

They said my daughter had doubtless run off with her boyfriend.

They always lied to us.

You have to remember how they put it to Doña Eva, whose daughter disappeared years ago and no one has gone after the ones who did it:

"Why look for her? Don't put your head in the lion's mouth."

And when we insisted, their answer was: "We'll see who gets tired of this first…"

When we got back home, a woman neighbor told us they had reported the discovery of a body with the same characteristics as Alejandra on TV.

Then I got a phone call confirming that the body they found had the clothes we described on the flyer.

I collapsed. They found me on the floor, crying, completely broken down, inconsolable.

The autopsy revealed that my daughter died on February 19.

Her body was half-naked and wrapped in a bedspread.

The local authorities received tips from witnesses who saw Ale being kidnapped by a group of men in a car, but they refused to investigate these testimonies in depth.

One lady saw how they hurriedly dragged her to a car and how she shouted, desperate, terrified. She fought and struggled. "Help! Help me, someone! Help!"

No one helped her.

The FBI from El Paso, Texas, has a report where someone recounts Alejandra's kidnapping in detail.

It was on Rancho El Becerro Street, and they put her into a white Thunderbird that was always parked in front of a nearby TV repair shop around the corner, where they took her later.

When they were kidnapping my daughter, when she resisted her "pick-up," they beat her and broke her nose.

The car was rocking as if someone inside were fighting, or as if a couple were having sex in it—that's what the witness said.

The owner of that shop is named Jorge and he's related to this guy, Raúl, who's a powerful drug dealer.

Raúl's gang mutilates their victims: men's testicles, girls' breasts.

Anyone who wants to work with them has to go through an initiation: kill whatever person they're ordered to, even someone from their own family.

This blood pact guarantees silence.

The authorities investigated the staff at that shop and said they "did not find evidence to establish any alleged responsibility."

Who believes them?

They didn't even accept that my daughter had been kidnapped: They insist she knew her attacker.

The FBI also reports on how girls are kidnapped downtown.

There's an individual involved they call "*El Licenciado*," who along with his assistant, a skinny, arrogant guy with a mustache, are the front for baiting the victims.

They approach girls who come into the music store on 16 de Septiembre Avenue, near the cathedral.

The girls go into the store and when they leave, young guys come up to them and start talking to them, they talk about the computer school twenty or thirty feet down the way, on the same street.

Somehow or another, the girls are fooled into going to *El Licenciado*'s nearby restaurant, where they attack and tie up the girls and then take them out into an alley where many prostitutes work.

The guy in charge of transporting the victims is called *El Güero* and he's the owner of another bar.

El Güero belongs to the drug cartel and operates out of a bunch of other dives.

He has an accomplice called *El Ritchie* whose job is to pay off the police to get rid of the bodies of the murdered girls. The authorities have never investigated these facts. My family had to confront all this without any help at all.

One day, by accident, my oldest daughter Malú discovered the photographs the forensic experts took of Alejandra's body. She was deeply affected. For some time she became aggressive and foul-mouthed and mistreated everyone.

My mother took refuge in fear. We had a lot of angry discussions. She said I should just let Alejandra rest in peace, that no matter what, her homicide would go unpunished, and she asked why I was looking for trouble by running around with other women in search of justice. She wanted to protect me.

Ever since Alejandra's death, José, my husband, changed completely. He used to be happy, strong, and he'd smile.

I remember a photograph they took of him when he was with Alejandra the day she turned fifteen and they cut the cake.

He was so happy. It was like when we met a long time ago. Then he became consumed with rancor, savage hatred, sadness. Every day he wanted to get into the trailer truck he drove, fill it with dynamite, and run it into the house where Alejandra's killers were.

A thirst for vengeance, fury, and impotence broke him down, little by little. He became very ill. One day they discovered terminal cancer.

We could only help him die decently.

Who pays for all this if the killers and the ones who protect them go free? They kidnapped my daughter, like so many other girls, right off the street.

They beat her.

They tied her hands.

They raped her.

They tortured her.

They mutilated her while she was alive.

They burned her with cigarettes.

They killed her by strangling her until she asphyxiated.

And then they threw her into a vacant lot like she was garbage.

Alejandra.

I looked at her in her coffin and I almost didn't recognize her: She who had had such a pretty, long neck was now like a hunchback, sunk down into her shoulders. They broke her. She faced an inhuman death all alone. She was just on her way home, like so many other girls.

Photograph 1

Portrait of the victim, Lilia Alejandra García Andrade, from a family album.

Photograph 2

Photo taken of Alejandra at the factory where she worked.

Photograph 3

Image taken from security cameras at the factory where Alejandra worked, the day of Alejandra's kidnapping on February 14, 2001, at the end of the workday, 7 PM.

Photograph 4

Bus stop, at the corner of Tecnológico and Ejército Nacional Avenues; Alejandra wears a woven black blouse with a closure at the neck, green pleated jeans, a black jacket with white stripes, white knee socks and black school shoes. Her physical description: seventeen years of age, light brown skin, large brown eyes, straight brown hair to the shoulders. 1.65 meters tall, approximately weighing 54 kg, straight nose, regular mouth, oval chin. She wears scapulars, a Timex watch with a vinyl band, a black Guess backpack.

Photograph 5

Alejandra resists abduction on Rancho Becerra
Street, not far from the plant where she worked.

Photograph 6

Alejandra's mother reports her disappearance at the Chihuahua State Judicial Police Missing Persons Bureau, 9:30 am, February 16.

Photograph 7

Printed notice of Alejandra's disappearance.

Photograph 8

Two individuals force a woman—Alejandra—into a white Thunderbird in front of a TV repair shop, the night of February 19, 2001.

Photograph 9

TV repair shop façade, property of an individual named Jorge.

Photograph 10

Rancho Agua Caliente Street, route taken by the Thunderbird.

Photograph 11

The discovery of Lilia Alejandra García Andrade's body by maintenance workers at the weed-filled vacant lot at the corner of Tecnológico and Ejército Nacional Avenues, 5 PM; the body is naked except for a black sweater and a brown scapular; the victim had been dead for approximately 24 hours.

Photograph 12

Alejandra's semi-hidden body as seen on television.

Photograph 13

The official in charge of the case declares that the investigations of Jorge and Raúl, pointed out as persons of interest in an FBI report made public in the press, "lack foundation and evidence."

Photograph 14

Alejandra's body, her neck fractured, with blows to the face, a mutilated nipple and marks indicating her hands were tied; 1.65 meters tall, regular complexion, light brown skinned *mestiza*, brown hair with some chemical treatment, 26 cm long, regular forehead, full eyebrows, brown eyes, concave nose, small mouth, exhibiting previous 4.5-centimeter surgery scars along the right flank, stretch marks along both sides of the abdomen as well as a dark infra-umbilical line; wears a black blouse with a zipper in the upper medium area, with a tear at the seam of the right sleeve, the rest of the garment lies at the level of the right armpit, no size or label is present, cinnamon-colored brassiere in place and fastened in the back, white socks with dark spots on the soles, a purple band on the right wrist, two brown religious-image scapulars about the neck; cause of death determined to be asphyxiation by strangulation occurring between 48 and 56 hours prior to the necropsy.

Photograph 15

Property at the corner of Tecnológico and Ejército Nacional Avenues, February 19, 2001.

Photograph 16

Property at the corner of Paseo de la Victoria and Prolongación de Ejército Nacional where, nine months later on November 6, 2001, eight murdered women were found in a cotton field.

Photograph 17

Alejandra's family, some years after her murder; her father is absent having died some time before.

Photograph 18

Satellite image of the property at Tecnológico and Ejército Nacional Avenues, February 14, 2001, 6:20 PM (31° 42' 21.21" N 106° 25' 13.02" W elev. 1119 m).

Photograph 19

Satellite image of the property at Tecnológico and Ejército Nacional Avenues, February 21, 2001, 7:00 PM (31° 42' 21.21" N 106° 25' 13.02" W elev. 1119 m).

Photograph 20

Satellite image of the property at Tecnológico and Ejército Nacional Avenues, February 14, 2001, 7:00 PM (31° 42' 21.21" N 106° 25' 13.02" W elev. 1119 m).

The previous account, based on case testimonies and documents, reconstructs the family environment of one victim: Lilia Alejandra García Andrade. She was kidnapped on a Ciudad Juárez street on February 14, 2001, as she left work at an assembly plant. She was discovered dead seven days later on February 21, in a vacant lot across from the Plaza Juárez Mall shopping center, a highly transited area. The autopsy revealed she died on February 19 of asphyxiation by strangulation. Her murder remains unpunished. Her mother, Norma Andrade, and a friend, Marisela Ortiz, founded the activist group *Nuestras Hijas de Regreso a Casa* ("Bring Our Daughters Home") in defense of the dozens of victims of the femicide machine. In 2011, the victim's sister, Malú Andrade, and Marisela Ortiz decided to leave Ciudad Juárez after receiving death threats.

On Friday, December 2, 2011, Norma Andrade was shot by a group of armed men while leaving work. The Chihuahua State Prosecutor's Office initially attributed the attack to a car-jacking. At the time of this printing, she remains in Ciudad Juárez under 24-hour protection.

In memory of Manuel Buendía, Enrique Camarena, Airis Estrella Enríquez Pando, Anai Orozco Lorenzo Lerma, Johana Radilla Sánchez, Marisela Escobedo, and the victims of the femicide machine.

Introduction

1. Gerald Raunig, *A Thousand Machines*, Semiotexte: Los Angeles, 2010, p. 33.

Chapter 1

1. http://mexico.cnn.com/historias-extraordinarias/2010/08/26/mexico-atrae-a-turistas-extremos-que-buscan-aventura-en-la-fron tera; Charles Bowden, *Murder City: Ciudad Juárez and the Global Economy's New Killing Fields*, New York: Nation Books, 2010.

2. http://www.unhabitat.org/.

3. Mike Davis, *Planet of Slums*, New York: Verso, 2007.

4. http://www.youtube.com/watch?v=JBaYKb3zfjo.

Chapter 2

1. http://www.ub.edu/geocrit/sn/sn119-53.htm.

2. Luis H. Méndez B., *Territorio, rito y símbolo. La industria maquiladora fronteriza*, Mexico City, *El Cotidiano*, March/April 2007, no. 142, UAM, pp. 10–15.

3. http://octavicomeron.net/ArteyPostfordismo.pdf.

4. http://www.revistasociologica.com.mx/pdf/5305.pdf, p. 147 and subsequent pages.

5. http://latribunadeensenada.com/?p=1436.

6. Giorgio Agamben, *Means Without End: Notes on Politics*, Minneapolis: University of Minnesota Press, 2000, p. 40.

7. http://www.jornada.unam.mx/2009/01/27/index.php?section=politica&article=009n1pol.

8. http://www.elfinanciero.com.mx/index.php/sociedad/corresponsales/13078-modifican-reglas-de-la-industria-maquiladora.

9. http://eleconomista.com.mx/notas-impreso/negocios/2009/05/20/mexico-maquila-mas-barato-que-china.

10. Mike Davis, *City of Quartz*, New York: Vintage Books, 1992, p. 4.

11. Andrés Oppenheimer, *Ojos vendados: Estados Unidos y el negocio de la corrupción en América Latina*, Mexico City: Plaza & Janés, 2001, p. 273.

12. http://mexico.cnn.com/nacional/2011/03/17/eu-tuvo-reportes-de-que-empresarios-contrataron-paramilitares-en-juárez.

13. http://www.senselab.ca/inflexions/volume_4/n4_introhtml.html.

14. http://www.santiago-sierra.com/200704_1024.php.

15. http://www.jhfc.duke.edu/icuss/pdfs/Mbembe.pdf.

Chapter 3

1. http://juárezland.wordpress.com/2010/12/02/revela-wikileaks-a-ciudad-juárez-como-proyecto-piloto-en-guerra-vs-narco/ and http://www.sedena.gob.mx/pdf/informes/tercer_informe_labores.pdf.

2. SIPRI Annual Report, June 2010, http://www.sipri.org/.

3. http://thereport.amnesty.org/sites/default/files/AIR2010_AZ_EN.pdf, page 170; pp. 223–226.

4. Diana Washington Valdez, *The Killing Fields: Harvest of Women*, Burbank: Peace at the Border, 2006, p. 281.

5. Charles Bowden, *Down By the River: Drugs, Money, Murder, and Family*, New York: Simon & Schuster, 2004.

6. http://www.fbi.gov/newyork/press-releases/2009/nyfo082009b.htm.

7. AFP, *Narcotraficantes que operan en México encuentran refugio en EU*, May 4, 2011: http://www.jornada.unam.mx/2011/05/04/index.php?section=politica&article=005n1pol.

8. http://www.todossomosjuárez.gob.mx/estrategia/avances/avances_al_28_de_junio_2010.pdf.

9. http://www.eluniversal.com.mx/nacion/164447.html.

10. Communiqué 185, Mexico's National Human Rights Commission, December 15, 2008, http://www.cndh.org.mx/comsoc/comsoc.asp.

11. http://mexico.cnn.com/nacional/2010/06/02/hasta-29000-mdd-del-narcotrafico-cruzan-anualmente-de-eu-a-mexico.

12. http://www.eluniversal.com.mx/primera/33939.html.

13. UN Office on Drugs and Crime, *La amenaza del narcotráfico en América*, October 2008, p. 13 and subsequent pages; Miguel Ángel Ortega, "*La conexión china de las tachas,*" *Contralínea* magazine, June 19, 2006. Electronic version: http://www.contralinea.com.mx/archivo/2004/julio.

14. UN Office on Drugs and Crime, *La amenaza del narcotráfico en América*, October 2008, p. 13 and subsequent pages; Miguel Ángel Ortega, "*La conexión china de las tachas,*" *Contralínea* magazine, June 19, 2006. Electronic text at: http://www.europol.europa.eu/publications/European_Organised_Crime_Threat_Assessment_(OCTA)/OCTA2009.pdf.

15. Homero Campa, "*Los Zetas y la Ndrangheta: La Conexión,*" *Proceso*, November 15, 2009, pp. 51–55.

16. *The Threat of Narco-Trafficking in the Americas*, United Nations/Office on Drugs and Crime, 2008, p. 31 and subsequent pages.

17. Moisés Naím, *Illicit: How Smugglers, Traffickers, and Copycats are Hijacking the Global Economy*, USA, Anchor, 2006, 352 pp.

18. http://www.aztecanoticias.com.mx/notas/mexico/27488/cndh-registra-65-periodistas-asesinados-en-10-anos.

19. http://www.diputados.gob.mx/cedia/sia/spe/SPE-ISS-02-06.pdf.

20. http://www.northcom.mil/about/index.html.

21. http://www.state.gov/secretary/rm/2009a/03/120905.htm; Jorge Carrasco A. y J. Jesús Esquivel, "*El Gran Espía*," *Proceso*, November 14, 2010, pp. 6–9.

22. "*71% del territorio nacional bajo control del narco*," *Proceso/Apro*, September 1, 2010; http://www.proceso.com.mx/rv/modHome/detalleExclusiva/82890.

23. http://www.unodc.org/documents/frontpage/UNODC_ Annual _Report_2010_LowRes.pdf.

24. http://www.eluniversal.com.mx/notas/745123.html.

25. http://www.bbc.co.uk/mundo/lg/internacional/2010/07/100728_mexico_eeuu_frontera_violencia_amab.shtml.

26. http://www.oem.com.mx/elsoldetijuana/notas/n606108.htm.

27. José Díaz Briseño, "*Pega a ATF escándalo por tráfico de armas*," Mexico, *Reforma*, March 5, 2011.

28. Bill Conroy, *U.S.-Backed Programs Supplying the Firepower for Mexico's Soaring Murder Rate*, April 14, 2011: http://narcosphere.narconews.com/notebook/bill-conroy/2011/04/us-backed-programs-supplying-firepower-mexico-s-soaring-murder-rate.

29. Fernández Menéndez, *op. cit.*, p. 24.

30. Mike Whitney, *Is the CIA behind Mexico's Bloody Drug War?*: http://www.globalresearch.ca/index.php?context=va&aid=18877.

31. Blanche Petrich, "*Intentó EU incluir en plan Mérida un acuerdo antiterrorista*," Mexico, "*La Jornada, una virtual amenaza terrorista [sic]*," February 12, 2011.

32. "*Piden en EU ver a narco como terrorismo*," Mexico, *Reforma*, March 31, 2011.

33. http://www.senado.gob.mx/sgsp/gaceta/61/2/2011-04-14-1/assets/documentos/ejecutivo.pdf.

34. J. Jaime Hernández, "*EU teme liga de Zetas y Al Qaeda*," Mexico, *El Universal*, February 10, 2011.

35. http://www.eluniversal.com.mx/nacion/184579.html; http://neglectedwar.com/blog/archives/5057.

36. http://www.eluniversal.com.mx/nacion/183668.html.

37. http://www.eluniversal.com.mx/nacion/162152.html and http://www.terra.com.mx/noticias/articulo/893154/Chapo+y+colombianos+lavan+dinero+en+Casa+de+Cambio+Puebla.htm.

38. Scott, *op. cit.*, locs. 1399–1405 and subsequent pages, Kindle edition.

39. Jorge Carrasco A. y J. Jesús Esquivel, *loc.cit.*

40. "*Entrenan mercenarios a soldados en País*," *Reforma*, April 6, 2011; Bill Conroy, *U.S. Private Sector Providing Drug-War Mercenaries to Mexico*, April 3, 2011, http://narcosphere.narconews.com/notebook/bill-conroy/2011/04/us-private-sector-providing-drug-war-mercenaries-mexico.

41. http://www.eluniversal.com.mx/notas/757697.html.

42. Oficina contra la Droga y el Delito, *La amenaza del narcotráfico en América Latina*, 2008, p. 3 and subsequent pages.

Chapter 4

1. *Informe de la Comisión de Expertos Internacionales de la Organización de las Naciones Unidas, Oficina de las Naciones Unidas contra la Droga y el Delito, sobre la Misión en Ciudad Juárez, Chihuahua, México*, November 2005, p. 2 and subsequent pages.

2. Julia Estela Monárrez Fragoso, *Trama de injusticia. Feminicidio sexual sistémico en Ciudad Juárez*, Tijuana, El Colegio de la Frontera Norte y Miguel Ángel Porrúa, 2009, p. 31.

3. Washington Valdez, *op. cit.*, pp. 235–240.

4. Rossana Reguillo, *La in-visibilidad resguardada: Violencia(s) y gestión de la paralegalidad en la era del colapso*, http://www.revistaalambre.com/Articulos/ArticuloMuestra.asp?Id=16.

5. Rita Laura Segato, *¿Qué es un feminicidio?* in Marisa Belausteguigoitia and Lucía Melgar's, *Fronteras, violencia, justicia: nuevos discursos,* Mexico City: UNAM, 2007, pp. 35–48.

6. Jane Caputi and Diana E. H. Russell, "Femicide: Sexist Terrorism against Women," in Jill Radford and Diana E. H. Russell, *Femicide: The Politics of Woman Killing,* New York: Twayne Publishers, 1992, p. 15.

7. Barbara Spinelli, *Femminicidio. Dalla denuncia sociale al riconoscimento giuridico internazionale,* Milan: FrancoAngeli, 2008.

8. *Plan Alternativo para solucionar el feminicidio en Ciudad Juárez,* Mexico City, PIEM-COLMEX/ PUEG-UNAM, 2005, 10 pp.

9. House of Representatives (*Cámara de Diputados*), Mexico City, 2007. http://www.diputados.gob.mx/LeyesBiblio/pdf/LGAMVLV.pdf.

10. Anmesty International, January 29, 2009, *México: a dos años de aprobada, ley de protección de mujeres sin impacto en estados,* agency bulletin, available here: http://www.amnesty.org/es/formedia/press-releases/mexico-dos-anos-ley-proteccion-mujeres-sin-impacto-20090129.

11. Rafael Arias, *La formalización de la realidad: noticia, acontecimiento mediático, ciberacontecimiento,* III Congreso Internacional de Periodismo en la Red, UCM, Madrid, 2008, p. 20.

12. http://www.corteidh.or.cr/docs/casos/articulos/seriec_205_esp.pdf.

13. Diana Washington Valdez, *op. cit.,* p. 375.

14. *Cities of Plain,* New York: Alfred A. Knopf, 1998, p. 285.

15. Cathy Fourez, in Belausteguigoitia and Melgar, *op. cit.,* p. 84.

BIBLIOGRAPHY

(B1) Anabel Hernández, *Los señores del narco*, Mexico City, Grijalbo, 2010, 587 pp.

(B2) Zygmunt Bauman, *Liquid Times: Living in an Age of Uncertainty*, UK, Polity, 2007, 128 pp.

(B3) Patrick Picouet and Jean-Pierre Renard, *Les frontières mondiales: Origines et dynamiques*, France, Editions du Temps, 2007, 159 pp.

(B4) Grace Livingstone, *America's Backyard: The United States and Latin America from the Monroe Doctrine to the War on Terror*, London, Zed Books, 2009, 256 pp.

(B5) Jorge Fernández Menéndez, *Narcotráfico y poder*, Mexico City, Rayuela Editores, 1999, 235 pp.

(B6) Peter Dale Scott, *American War Machine: Deep Politics, the CIA Global Drug Connection, and the Road to Afghanistan*, USA, Rowman & Littlefield Publishers, 2010, 408 pp./Kindle Edition.

semiotext(e) intervention series